Reflections for Everyday Life

"*Show me O Lord, Your Way*"
Psalms 27:11

Deacon Anthony C. Bonacci

Reflections for Everyday Life

Deacon Anthony C. Bonacci

Plain City, Ohio

ISBN: 978-1-945423-25-3 (Paperback)

Front cover artist and design consultant: Emma Lentz

Book Layout by the International Localization Network Staff

Printed in the United States of America.

First Printing edition 2021 Five Stones Publising

A division of:
The International Localization Network
109 Sunset Court #2
Hamburg, NY 14075

Dedication

To my four children, Lynn, Tina, Maria, and Anthony; and to my eight grandchildren, Kelsey, Christopher, Emma, Andrew, Noah, Logan, Jonah, and Carmen.

May the Lord guide, guard, and protect you always.

Acknowledgements

Thanks to a special friend and parishioner, Mrs. Shirley Tornik, for proof-reading and critiquing the manuscript.

Thanks to Father Patrick Toner, Deacon Frank Iannarino, and parishioner Mrs. Lori Crock for reviewing and commenting on the manuscript.

Thanks also to my granddaughter, Miss Emma Lentz, a college student in Visual Communications Design at Kent State University, for designing and creative input for the book and book cover.

Contents

Forward

"Receive the gospel of Christ whose herald you now are. Believe what you read, teach what you believe, and practice what you teach." These words of mission are said by the Bishop during the ordination Mass for a deacon in the Roman Catholic tradition. They are said as the newly ordained deacon kneels before the Bishop who then places the Book of the Gospels in his hands. It is a gesture that signifies a solemn moment of commissioning for the new clergyman. He is to be grounded in the gospel by studying it faithfully, allowing its truth to resonate into every part of his life, and then witnessing that truth to others by the way he lives his life.

In "*Reflections for Everyday Life*", Deacon Bonacci breaks open the Word of God as found in the Sunday Gospels of the Roman Catholic Church throughout the liturgical seasons. He provides the reader with a relatable and relevant application of the gospel message just as he has provided his parishioners for nearly a quarter-century. His words have enriched his parishioners' faith life and given them spiritual food for active living. They have often remarked how they could readily take his relevant messages from the pew to their homes and their workplaces.

The insights in this book are forged from Deacon Tony's varied background, reflecting the life of one who has tasted life's trials as well as its joys. His writing is forged by his life experiences. Tony grew up on the South side of Buffalo, a blue-collar neighborhood which bordered Lake Erie, and which was known for its two behemoth steel plants and supporting industries. He lost his father at a very young age but his mother remarried and brought him a wonderful second father as well as younger siblings.

Deacon Tony excelled academically under the guidance of the Sisters of Mercy at Holy Family School and the Franciscan Friars at Bishop Timon High School. At the University of Buffalo he earned a B.Sc. degree in pharmacy, followed by an M.Sc. degree at The Ohio State University. There he practiced hospital pharmacy and taught at the College of Pharmacy for over thirty years. Along the way he married the love of his life, Elainc, and they were blessed with four children and eight grandchildren.

After 53 years of marriage, he again experienced the pain of loss and had to say farewell to Elaine, who was not only his wife but his spiritual companion. His writings and homilies were often touched by her wisdom and insight.

I have often heard it said that there are no "coincidences," only "God-incidents," and that is not wasted on my history with Deacon Bonacci. We grew up on the same street and went to the same elementary school, but our four-year age difference meant we played with different kids. Our paths had crossed many times, but we didn't realize it until many years later when we both worked at The Ohio State University.

One afternoon shortly after I was ordained a deacon, Tony (who had an interest in the diaconate) was encouraged to speak to me about the program. I will forever remember our amusing exchange, when Tony said I "didn't speak like I was from Ohio," and that I had a familiar accent. I told him I was from Buffalo. "Oh Yea, I'm from Buffalo too," he responded. I continued, "I'm from the South side." He said, "I'm from the South side too, Woodside and South Park." "Me too," I exclaimed, and we had a great laugh catching up on life and how God brought us together. He went on to be my brother deacon, and his wisdom and deep spirituality have enriched my life. This book will enrich yours.

Deacon Phil Paulucci
Diocese of Columbus

Preface

My first book, *Faith, Family, and Formation*, sub-titled *God's Plan Revealed*, was the result of a "perfect storm" and the suggestion of two dear friends.

The "perfect storm" included: first, a long dry summer when there was little time needed for the yard; second, the "Covid-19" pandemic, which meant isolation and separation from others; and third, the recent passing of my dear wife Elaine.

Two friends suggested, "You ought to write a book" after hearing of several of my life experiences, either as part of a homily or in private discussion.

It seems that other happenings also contributed to my decision to author my first book: first, my decision to review and sort thousands of photographs collected over seventy-plus years; second, the realization that God has a plan for my life, has perfect timing, and has been in control of my life through all its (temporary) trials and tribulations; and third, my desire to leave a legacy for my descendants.

In this volume, I offer reflections based on homilies I have presented during my 24 years as a Catholic deacon. Many times, I share true stories or experiences that illustrate the theme of the homily. Looking back, I now realize that my life experiences have prepared me for my preaching ministry. I am convinced that God wants me to continue writing for the rest of my days and proclaim the gospel by sharing reflections based on my homilies.

As I enter my twenty-fifth year of ministry, my hope and prayer is that the reader will be reminded of similar situations in his/her life, will be encouraged to apply the lesson of the cited scriptures to their own life, and will be motivated to carry on according to God's holy and perfect will.

At the time I am writing this book, our country is dealing with the Covid-19 pandemic, unprecedented divisiveness after a national election, and serious issues in the Catholic Church. The pandemic has taken the lives of over 350,000 people in the U.S. alone and has seriously affected our economy. The political wrangling over the presidential election continues. Catholic clergy are aging, over-worked, and losing credibility.

It is my hope and prayer that the pandemic will end, that political divisiveness will be resolved, and that clergy and laity will work together to return the Church to Truth, transparency, and accountability.

Cycle A Reflections
(Based on Sunday Gospels for Cycle A)

"Show me O Lord, Your Way"

(Psalm 27:11)

Preparing for the Lord's Coming

Matt.24:37-44

"Be alert!" they tell us; "be prepared!" they say. Ever since "9-11" in 2001, our public officials have reminded us that terrorism can occur at any moment. They tell us, "We know it's coming; we just don't know when." So we prepare. We increase security everywhere, even in our schools and in our churches. We prepare vaccines; we irradiate the mail; we monitor communications.

Ever since the 2020 Covid-19 pandemic broke out, these same officials have asked us to wear face masks, wash our hands often, and practice "social distancing."

Our officials are not threatening us; they're teaching us to be vigilant, to protect ourselves and others, and to be prepared!

In this passage from Matthew, Jesus says, "Be alert! Be prepared." Jesus is not threatening us; he's teaching us. He's teaching us to be alert, to prepare for His coming; to prepare for our passing!

We know He's coming! We pray in the creed, "He will come again to judge the living and the dead..." We just don't know when! Just consider the events of recent years: the political events, the technological events, the environmental events, and the weather events. it seems to many people that God's plan for the world is   s-l-o-w-l-y unfolding... God's plan to bring all of creation into unity with Him.

And if Jesus doesn't come in our lifetime, that means He'll be calling us (you and me) before he comes back. Either way, the only sensible thing to do, is be ready, be prepared!

"Being prepared." It's not a stressful way to live; it's a good way to live! It gives life purpose; it gives life meaning!

The whole reason we're here is to prepare for the Lord's coming, whether He comes in majesty first, or whether He calls us home first.

So, how do we prepare for the Lord's coming?

We prepare:

-by **praying**, praising & worshipping God;

-by **reconciling** with that relative or friend who offended us, instead of nursing a grudge; **LET IT GO!**

-by being **gentle** with the people who cross our path;

-by **visiting** or **transporting** that ill or elderly person, instead of driving right past their street;

-by **sharing** some of our material blessings with the needy, instead of always striving to get more, bigger, stuff!

Preparing for the Lord's coming - one of the most beautiful prayers in the Mass is right after the Our Father, when the priest says, "...We await the blessed hope and the coming of our Savior…"

Jesus wants us to prepare for his coming. Jesus wants us to prepare a place for him – in our heart!

Jesus wants us to live "in blessed hope," alert for the signs of his second coming… but prepared for the possibility of His calling us home first.

God's Timetable

James 5:7-10
Matt.11:2-11

Did you ever pray for patience? What happened? I've found that's when everything seems to break loose! Maybe that's how God teaches us patience. The point is:

Things happen by God's timetable - not ours.

James urges the early Christians to be patient with God's timetable. James is saying, "Look, we don't know when the Lord is coming, but we shouldn't be impatient. And if we're frustrated by the waiting, we shouldn't take it out on each other. We should be hopeful and not grouchy."

Do I get impatient with waiting? Do I get impatient with suffering, with setbacks in my plans, with mechanical things that break or wear out? Do I sometimes take it out on others? The most hurtful impatience comes when we take it out on those we love – on our own family members.

We're just like the early Christians: We need encouragement. We need reassurance that God is always there: when there's illness, when there's job problems, when there's family troubles. Sometimes, we feel like crying out, "God, give me patience!" But **things happen by God's timetable, not ours.**

"Patience" - even the word sounds peaceful… Patience is a calmness in waiting. Patience is a calmness in bearing pain or misfortune. Patience implies courage in tough times.

Patience is enduring life, with all the ups and downs it brings. Patience is having hope and a positive vision for the future, like the prophet Isaiah describes. Patience is longing for His second coming. "Thy kingdom come…" – where there's no suffering, no illness, no violence, no hunger, and no homelessness.

For example, the season of Advent is a time for patience. Advent means "coming," the coming of the Lord at His birth. It's a time to wait patiently and prepare carefully. During Advent, We learn that God's timetable is not our timetable. We learn that God fulfills His word in his own good time, and that He will come in his own good time.

Each time we receive the Eucharist, we prepare our hearts for the coming of our Savior, asking for the joy of His presence, and asking for patience with God's timetable.

Receiving Jesus

Many of us are parents, grandparents, or Godparents. Remember for a moment how it felt when they first put a newborn baby in your arms… your child, or grandchild, or Godchild… the feelings of warmth and wonder; the feeling of gratitude for that new life…

Imagine Simeon - this holy old man who had been waiting in the temple for years, for the Messiah! How he longed to see the Messiah before he died, and his prayer was answered! What an honor! - To receive in his arms, the Christ child, the Savior of His people! Can you imagine the joy in his heart?

Now imagine Mary and Joseph, observant Jews, who bring the baby Jesus to the temple to be consecrated to the Lord - a sign that He would serve God throughout His life.

And imagine Joseph! Foster father of Jesus, leader of the holy family, a man of faith and determination, a man's man! Joseph says not one word that's recorded in the gospels, yet we can perceive his great faith – faith that God would protect his family if he followed God's will. Simeon prophesies, says that Jesus will be "a light for revelation to the Gentiles"…

At every Mass, we hear the words, "Behold the Lamb of God, who takes away the sin of the world." **Behold**: don't just glance! Behold! Look deeply, carefully, and prayerfully! **The Lamb of God**: Jesus, the one true sacrifice sent from heaven, the spotless Lamb! **who takes away sin**: the promise of forgiveness! …**of the world**: the sin of every single person on earth, past, present, and future!

More than one of us have had a non-Catholic friend say, "You know, if I believed as you Catholics do, that Jesus Christ is really present in that consecrated bread and wine, in that tabernacle, in that monstrance at adoration, I would be in church all the time (24/7), on my knees, or lying prostrate before Him!"

I will always remember bringing Holy Communion to one particular lady in medical intensive care. After she devoutly received the Eucharist, she looked me in the eye and said, "Who am I...who am I that I can receive my Lord and Savior into my body and into my heart?"

Just think! You and I have the privilege and joy of receiving Jesus, cradling Jesus in our hand or on our tongue every time we receive Holy Communion. We have the privilege of visiting Him at Adoration and Exposition of the Blessed Sacrament. Most of all, we have the privilege of His constant presence: in His Word, in His minister, in the Eucharist, and in each other!

At Mass, may we devoutly cradle Him and devoutly receive Him into our body and into our heart!

Seasoning and Light for the World

Matt. 5: 13-16

Salt is a simple seasoning. It flavors our food. And it preserves food.

Light brightens our lives. it helps us to see things.

Salt... **light**... Jesus gives us two simple images to guide our lives, images to define our mission. He says, "You are the salt of the earth!" He's saying, "You season the lives of others, you flavor the world, you improve the quality of life! You preserve the world!"

How? By our actions!

He says, "You are the light of the world!" He's saying, "You brighten the world, you define who we are as Christians! You help people to "see" God!"

How? By our actions!

It's a simple message! Everyone can understand it (whether we're six or sixty). Our actions improve the quality of life. They bring hope to our darkened world. I will always remember the teenagers at the Right to Life walks in Washington, D.C. every year. These young people are saying, "We're going to change this world for the better! We're not going to stand for some of this evil stuff that's going on!" These young people are "salt of the earth;" these young people are "light of the world!"

How can we be "salt of the earth," how can we be "light of the world," what actions can we take, here, where we are? Isaiah tells us, "Do not turn your back on your own."

We can *season* - season our marriage relationship with a sincere compliment, by doing something without being asked, by letting the small stuff pass;

We can *preserve* - preserve the self-image of that teenager in our life by respecting their opinions, by a little more listening and a little less nagging.

We can *shed light* - shed light on a friend or co-worker's problem by just listening, or by a sincere comment that shows we care.

We are salt; we are light. It's our mission as Christ's disciples!

We "season" by what we say and do; by the way we say it and the way we do it. We "preserve" by our compassion, by our encouragement. We "enlighten" by offering hope to those in despair, or to those who are bereaved.

And why should we do this? To get a gold "star" in God's big scorebook? Or so that someone will say, "My, my, isn't Mary a wonderful person?" Jesus says, "...so that others, upon seeing our good deeds, will praise and glorify our heavenly Father." That's why we do it! We do it so that someone will say, "my, my, isn't God wonderful!"

Jesus says, "(name), you are the world's seasoning. Season and flavor the lives of others."

"(name), please help me to preserve this world."

"(name), you are the world's light- as a Christian, you're like a city on a hill, glowing in the night. Don't hide your light!"

"(name), let your good deeds glow, so that others will praise your heavenly Father!"

Let's ask ourselves, "Who in my family needs a kind word from me? Who's that young person in my life who needs some encouragement, or a pat on the back? Who at work needs my support, or some help with a problem? Who's that student at school who needs a warm hug? Who's that child who needs some guidance? Who's that ill person at church who needs some assurance, or just a caring smile? Who's that lonely neighbor who needs some company?

It's our mission to season and preserve the lives of others; it's our mission to bring light and hope to our darkened world; and most importantly, it's our mission to bring praise to almighty God.

Don't lose your flavor! We make the world tolerable for each other! Don't hide your light! We light the way for each other!

Loving Relationships

"Do you love me?" says Tevye repeatedly. Many of us remember the familiar, heart-warming dialogue between Tevye and Golde, husband and wife in the play "*Fiddler on the Roof.*" For Golde, love is a decision. She loves with her head, she loves with her heart, and she loves with her actions. When you think about it, in marriage and in all relationships, love is a decision! As Christians, We are called to make this decision; we are called to loving relationships.

In Matthew's gospel, Jesus is tempted; tempted to break his loving relationship with God the Father. Satan tempts Jesus with pleasure, power and possessions. Pleasure, power, and possessions: the same temptations that we have; the same temptations that tear at all relationships – husband/wife; friend/friend; parent/child; brother/sister; even our relationship with God.

It seems that Satan is always there, trying to tear us apart, trying to destroy our loving relationships. Believe it! Satan is real; he's not a joke or a fairy tale! Satan is never happier than when he splits couples, destroys friendships, estranges siblings, alienates child from parent, or separates us from God! Satan attacks Christian relationships!

You might be thinking, "Hey, if Jesus is God, why did He allow himself to be tempted by Satan?" With a snap of his finger, He could have cast Satan right back into hell! But Jesus allowed it; allowed it to set an example for us - how to resist temptation. Jesus uses prayer and the word of God to resist Satan's temptations.

We have prayer, we have the word of God, and what's more, we have the sacraments. We have self-disciplines, like fasting and abstaining; we have almsgiving; we have spiritual direction; and we have other Christians around us. We have remedies for sin and temptation. By the way, temptation

Deacon Anthony C. Bonacci   19

is not a sin! Even Jesus was tempted by the devil. It's when we agree, when we choose, to do wrong, that it becomes a sin.

We are called to reject Satan and make love a decision, We are called to make loving relationships a decision. We are called to do whatever it takes to nourish our relationships. It may require patience or forgiveness, or letting go of a grudge, or over-looking a shortcoming…it may call for the sacrament of reconciliation.

Let us use these remedies for sin and temptation (prayer, the word, the Eucharist, self-discipline, and almsgiving) as power - power to reject Satan. It works! But it's not easy! It takes effort!

As we approach the Eucharist, our spiritual food, our source of power and strength, may we commit to loving relationships – with each other, and with almighty God.

Recipe for Happiness

Matt. 5: 1-12

In the summer of 1985, a young lady gave a graduation speech. As she looked out at her classmates, she said, "Whatever our plans, each of us is seeking the same thing - happiness." "For us," she said, 'happiness' is an exciting new life: in college, or in the military, or in married life...."

Often, when I preach at weddings, the couple chooses the beatitudes for their wedding gospel. All couples seek the same thing - happiness.

Immanuel Kant, the great philosopher, said that happiness is "...having something to do, someone to love, and something to look forward to." So what about us? What makes us happy? Our society tells us it's a new car, or a fast computer, or clothes from Abercrombie & Fitch, or a vacation to Hawaii. Fine, but even if we attain some of these things, we soon learn that material things don't bring lasting happiness. Maybe happiness is a less hectic life style, or good health, or being surrounded by those we love, or just a sense of peace with God and with others.

God wants us to be happy - now and for all eternity. In Matthew's gospel he gives us the recipe for happiness: the Beatitudes - Jesus' teachings of what happiness is, and how and when to achieve it. But isn't this an odd list? "Happy are the poor, the sorrowful, the lowly, the hungry?" it's not a list we would make, is it?

Yet the beatitudes are a way of life for the Christian. Let's look at two of them:

"Blessed are the poor in spirit, for theirs is the kingdom of heaven." "Poor" here does not mean a lacking, but a seeking. We are "poor in spirit" when we know we have to depend on God, when we turn to God for help:

-maybe we're sitting in a doctor's office, waiting for the results of a test (what if he tells me.......?);

-maybe we're sitting in the boss's office, and we've just heard that the company has been bought out. (what if I lose my job?).

-maybe we're sitting at home in bad weather, and we're anxious about the safety of someone we love. In times like these, we are "poor in spirit." We know we have to depend on God. We humble ourselves and look to God for happiness. We humble ourselves and we are truly "blessed."

"Blessed are the clean of heart, for they shall see God." We are "clean of heart," or "single-hearted," when we center our lives on God;

-when we realize that true riches are found only in God (and so we share what we have);

-when we discover that true joy is found only in God (and so in times of sorrow, we draw closer to him);

-when we understand that only God can lift the lowly (and so we admit that we can't do it ourselves);

-when we show mercy to someone who's offended us (and so we forgive instead of holding a grudge);

-when we promote peace among our friends (and so we help to settle a disagreement)

-when we even accept suffering as part of being a Christian. When we are "single-hearted," we are disciples of Jesus, and we are truly "blessed."

Jesus practiced what he preached. The beatitudes are a description of Christ himself! When we imitate Him, We are truly "blessed."

Each one of the Beatitudes could stand by itself, and yet there's a unity among them - the promise of lasting happiness, the joy of living in God's presence. The beatitudes offer us hope for the future. They uplift us when we feel defeated. They offer the encouragement of final reward.

May we humble ourselves and look to God for happiness. The happiness we feel on earth is only a sampling of the full, perfect, and permanent joy that awaits us in heaven.

Preparing for the Passage

Luke 9: 28-36
Phil. 3:17-4,1

One of my previous pastors asked, "Who wants to go to heaven?" (All hands went up.) Then he said, "Now, here's a tougher question: who wants to die to get there?" (No hands went up.)

Getting to heaven involves a journey, a journey we call "life." Getting to heaven involves a passage, a passage we call "death."

In Luke's gospel, Jesus takes Peter, James, and John up the mountain. While he's praying, He is transfigured before them. He is transformed. His face shines like the sun, and his clothes become dazzling white. Jesus gives a glimpse of heavenly life.

Heaven; heaven is our destiny! St. Paul says, "He will transform our lowly bodies to be like His glorious body." We can look forward to a place with no heart disease, no cancer, no Alzheimer's disease, no arthritis or diabetes, and no addictions. These mortal bodies of ours are a beautiful handiwork of God, yet they're prone to disease, breakdown, and death. They can't enter heaven without a transformation.

So how do we prepare for this change? How should we act and think as Catholic Christians making the journey, preparing for the passage?

-first, by holding fast to God's promises. St. Paul says, "Stand firm in the Lord." He's saying, "Keep the faith! Ride out the hills and valleys that are part of life."

-second, by not getting side-tracked by the things of the world (all the stuff). The human condition is temporary! Money, houses, cars, clothes, power, position - it's all temporary! We can't anticipate heaven if we're absorbed in things.

Deacon Anthony C. Bonacci

23

-third, by demonstrating our Christianity. St. Paul says, "Live a life centered in Christ." We might say, "but life is so busy, so complicated... what can we do?"

- We can spend a few minutes each day in personal prayer, even in the car; we can spend a few minutes before the Blessed Sacrament;

- We can observe a time of fasting or self-denial; we can give some thing or some time to the poor;

- We can try to root out a particular sin;

- We can turn off the TV, and read something that renews our spirit, like mother Teresa, or Henri Nouwen, or Father Cedric Pisegna;

- We can meditate on the Transfiguration, thinking of our deceased loved ones. A meditation like this brings us closer to our deceased loved ones, and reduces our fear of death.

In the Transfiguration, Jesus shows Himself bright and powerful, to encourage us to face the ups and downs of everyday life. In the transfiguration, Jesus gives us faith and hope in our future glory.

There is glory, but to achieve it, we must undergo a passage. We may not want to go through that portal, but go we must, We have no choice.

But we're not alone! And we need not be afraid! We have each other! We have our faith community, and above all, we have Jesus, who's been through it all, who knows what it's all about, who walks with us on the journey.

May we rejoice as we continue the journey, as we prepare for the passage!

Called to God's Service

Acts 10:34-38
Matt.3:13-17

There once was a song on Christian radio, and the lyrics included:

"…if we are the body [of Christ], why aren't His arms reaching, why aren't His hands healing, why aren't His words teaching… and if we are the body, why aren't His feet going, why is His love not showing them there is a way?"

If we are the body of Christ, we have to reach out, heal, teach, move our feet sometimes, and we have to use love to show them "there is a way, there is a way." As Christians, it's our job to be the hands, and feet, and lips of Christ.

In the gospel of Matthew, Jesus is baptized to begin his public ministry. Through our baptism, we receive a call to ministry, a call to serve God and others. God calls each of us to a vocation, a way of life, a state in life.

"Vocation" - the word means "a calling." All vocations are a calling from God. Whether single, married, clergy, or consecrated religious life, all vocations are "callings" from God.

We should reflect on and celebrate our own vocation; we should reflect on our children's choice of a vocation. As good parents, we'll be there to help them choose a career, i.e., a profession, but how about helping them choose their vocation? As good parents, we are concerned that they decide what they will do with their lives (their career); but we also need to give time and attention to what they will be (their vocation).

So how can we help them decide? First, we can teach our children that each person is called to God's service; we can make them aware of all four vocations open to them; we can point out the gifts and talents God has given them; we can teach them to pray and listen for God's guidance in their choice of a vocation; We can encourage them to ask questions, answer their questions (or get the answers for them). In these ways, We can help them decide how God may be calling them.

Deciding on a career is not easy. There are so many choices. Discerning God's call to a vocation and living that call is not easy either. Parents need to invest some time in this and discuss vocation options with their children.

Through our baptism, each of us receives a call. God calls us to his service through our vocation. Each of us responds, serving God and others, as a single person, as a married couple, or as consecrated religious or clergy.

May you and your children rejoice in your vocation!

The Desert, the Devil, and Decision
Matt.4:1-11

On Good Friday, 1972, I received a long distance call, and I heard three words one never wants to hear: "Mom has cancer." It was the beginning of a 5-yr. struggle for my Dad, my siblings and our young families - it was like a walk through the desert. It was a time of pain and a time of doubt.

Five years later, at Easter, we still felt like we were alone in the desert. We knelt in the church where we grew up, and asked God, "If it's Your will, please take her home; we don't want her to suffer any more." God took her home that summer.

Jesus walked alone in the desert. In the gospel of Matthew, Satan tempted him with pleasure, power, and riches - the same ways he tempts us. He told Jesus, "Turn these stones into bread!" Satan tempts us, "Go ahead, indulge yourself; you deserve it!" (food, alcohol, nicotine; work-aholism; worshipping at the mall; juicy gossip; trashy TV; pornography). Satan told Jesus, "Throw yourself down from the steeple!" He tempts us, "Go ahead, promote yourself, show them your power and your importance!"

Satan told Jesus, "Worship me, and I'll give you all the kingdoms of the earth!" He tempts us, "Follow earthly ways, and you'll get rich quick!"

We call him "Satan" or "the devil" or "Lucifer" or "the evil one." It's a fact: the devil is real! He's not a joke or a fairy tale.

Every temptation seems good. It wasn't easy for Jesus, either. But he's our model. In the desert, He decided not to be self-indulgent; He decided not to display his power; He decided not to partner with the devil for riches.

The desert, the devil, and decision: it's our choice how we respond to temptations, and we are responsible for our choices. We can't blame others; we can't blame our jobs or our busy schedules; we can't even blame the devil. He's the source of evil, and he urges us to evil, but the decision to sin is ours!

We need to think about our choices. We need to get down to basics. We need to ask ourselves: "What are my temptations?; How do I sin?; Whom do I need to forgive?; From whom do I need to ask forgiveness?

We all walk through deserts – painful, lonely deserts. The devil is there, inserting doubt and division. Satan is never happier than when he sows division between husband and wife, between parent and child, between brother and sister, between friend and friend, and especially between us and God. Believe it!

In the desert, Jesus decided against Satan's temptations, and angels ministered to Him. He offers us help in our walks through the desert, in our defiance of the devil, and in our decisions for Christ. He offers us the sacraments, especially Penance and the Eucharist. He offers us the Word of God and personal prayer. He offers Himself as the model, and He offers us angels to minister to us!

Christt Our Light

John 9:1-41

Light is so important in our life!

We need light to look at our life, to see all the events in our life. We need light to get through the dark stretches (the trials and troubles) in our life; we need light to understand that they're not punishments.

We need light to find our way back from side roads where we can get lost. Maybe it's a rush for status and "stuff;" maybe we've drifted away from the Church.

We need light to get rid of blind spots, like opinions or habits we don't like questioned!

We need the light of knowledge to answer questions, like, "Oh, what's wrong with abortion, anyway? It's just a blob of tissue!" Or, "What's the big deal with you Catholics and capital punishment?

We need light to recognize the miracles in our life, like the everyday miracles of nature; the birth of a baby; all those "coincidences" that happen (those "God-incidences").

We need light to understand the signs; some big, some small - those special directions from God.

We need light to recognize the special people crossing our path, sometimes more than once! They help us, urge us, support us, and comfort us.

We need light to see our way when we pause and try to figure out where we are, or where we really want to go in life.

So where is this "light"? Who is this light? *Jesus* is the light! - The light who first shines on us in Baptism; the light who helps us to see the Father. St. Paul says, "There was a time when we were in darkness, but now we are light in the Lord."

John tells us about the miracle of the blind man: he receives not only physical sight, but spiritual sight. He goes from blindness, to "sight," to insight! His faith develops gradually, his insight comes slowly, just like ours! He represents each one of us.

We are like David; we are "chosen." We are like the blind man; we are "sent." God chooses and sends each of us to be his ministers in this world: to receive the light, and to be light to others.

Our life is a short spiritual journey. We're all in different places along the "way." The important thing to remember is that the light is always there! Sometimes, He's ahead, leading. Sometimes, he's behind, pushing. Sometimes, he's alongside, accompanying. And sometimes, he carries us.

Faith and Hope in Eternal Life

John 11:3-7,17,20-27,33-45

There's something peaceful about walking in a cemetery: viewing the monuments and markers, reading the names and dates. The inscriptions are inspiring; my favorite one is, "*God be with you 'till we meet again.*" Walking in the cemetery brings back memories, memories of loved ones who have passed on. Most importantly, it gives one faith and hope in eternal life, the theme of this reading from John: faith and hope in eternal life.

In this gospel, Jesus says, "*I am the resurrection and the life. Whoever believes in me, even if he dies, will live, and everyone who lives and believes in me will never die.*"

Powerful words! Words that motivate us to believe in eternal life; to expect eternal life; to prepare for eternal life; even yearn for eternal life!

I look forward to re-uniting with my wife Elaine, meeting my father who died when I was three years old; re-uniting with my Dad "Ted," who became my "Papa" since I was five; my Mom Connie who died (way too young) at age 59 of cancer; aunts & uncles, grandparents, the good Sisters who taught me in elementary school, the Franciscan Friars who taught me in high school, friends and neighbors, and professional colleagues.

"*Lazarus - Come forth!*" Jesus says. Lazarus represents every Christian, because every Christian is called to die and rise with Christ. Someday, when you or I pass on, the people of God will pray, "Eternal rest grant unto him(her), O Lord." The people of God are really praying, "Eternal *life* grant unto him(her), O Lord."

Lazarus represents every Christian, because every Christian is called to be set free from the bindings of sin, to be loosed by the Sacrament of Penance.

Here's the point: The ultimate choice we make is the choice between "life" and "death." We choose a life of fellowship with God and others; or, we choose death - the death of separation from God and others. We choose Christ-centered lives directed toward others; or, we choose self-centered lives without Christ. It's our choice.

At every Mass, the priest drops a piece of the sacred, consecrated Host into the precious Blood as he prays, "May this mingling of the body and blood of Our Lord Jesus Christ bring eternal life to us who receive it."

Jesus' clear teachings and Jesus' bold actions give us faith and hope in eternal life. God's love is our guarantee of eternal life. God alone has the power to keep us, His loved ones, forever. If we choose to embrace Him, He will never, ever let us go! And when our earthly life ends, may Jesus be there, holding out His hand, calling us by name. May we hear His gentle words, *My beloved, come forth! My beloved, come home.*"

Recognizing Him

Luke 24:13-35

In Luke's gospel, two disappointed disciples leaving Jerusalem are upset that Jesus has been crucified. Puzzled by the events, and by rumors that He had "risen from the dead," they're in deep discussion when a "stranger" joins them. (The "stranger" of course, is Jesus, who they don't recognize.) The "Stranger" gently reveals Himself to them and their eyes are opened; their hearts "burn" inside them, yet they still haven't recognized Him!

They arrive at their destination, and insist that He spend the night. They share a meal, and at table, Jesus "took bread, said the blessing, broke it, and gave it to them..." And they *recognize* Him "in the breaking of the bread."

There are eleven accounts of Resurrection appearances in the Bible. This must be one of the most beautiful! - Jesus making Himself known by opening the scriptures and breaking the bread: Word and Sacrament marking His presence.

Luke tells us that the one disciple was named "Cleopas." He doesn't tell us the name of the other person. Maybe we're that other disciple, we who gather in community to open the Word of God, to "break the bread." Maybe this Word and this altar is our Emmaus!

When we open the Word, we see what God has done in order to understand what God is doing now. We listen to what God said so we can understand what God is saying now. God's words and actions of the past become present among us!

Our Liturgy of the Word is followed by a meal: The risen Christ alive and present in the Eucharist. The Word touches our mind; The Eucharist touches and becomes part of our body. Just think! Every time we celebrate the Eucharist, we celebrate the life, death, and Resurrection of Jesus, and our own life, death, and resurrection. And here's the best part:

Deacon Anthony C. Bonacci   *33*

We celebrate in Community! We recognize Christ in each other - not just at the sign of peace, but after we leave the church and go off to our families, friends, classmates, and co-workers. We recognize Christ even in "strangers."

Two disciples on the road to Emmaus showed hospitality to a "Stranger" - hospitality that led them to recognize Christ! Our hospitality, our openness, to Christ leads us to recognize Him: in the Word, in the Eucharist, and in each other!

We Glorify God

John 17:1-11a

We are God's glory in the world! We reflect God's beauty, we reflect God's magnificence to the world.

At Mass, we say, "Glory to God in the highest…Lord God, heavenly King, almighty God and Father…" We recognize God's divinity. We recognize God's presence.

At the Last Supper, Jesus prays that the Father will glorify Him as He has glorified the Father. Jesus has made the Father's presence known.

Jesus prays for His disciples – His disciples then and His disciples now. He has taught them, led them, and now they understand His mission and His message. They know God in the Son He has sent; they accept "eternal life." And so Jesus passes the baton, this mission to glorify the Father, to make God's presence known. As He does, He prays for them and He prays for us. The world will resist them; the world will resist us!

So how do we do it? How do we take the baton and carry on the mission to glorify the Father? We do it by doing what Jesus did:

First, we dare to live life fully. Father John Powell once said we must "accept ourselves; be ourselves; forget ourselves in love to others; believe, and belong." We glorify God by living life fully!

Second, we live Christ-like lives. Like Jesus, we blend gentleness and strength. We form ourselves into a person who shines for others, a person who reflects God's glory. We glorify God by living Christ-like lives!

Third, we minister to others. We serve others. We help them live life to the full. Whenever we use our talents, creativity, and gifts to do as Jesus did, we are "ministers." In the Cursillo movement, we say "We are the hands and feet and lips of Christ." We glorify God when we minister to others!

Fourth, we pray. In your heart and in my heart, in the heart of every human being, there is a hunger to know God. We know God by conversing with Him in prayer, both speaking and listening. God wants to share our joys, our sorrows, our efforts, our temptations, and even our feelings. There are so many kinds and styles of prayer, so many forms of prayer. We pray for so many people and situations. Some of us keep a "prayer list." And sometimes, prayer is waiting for God to act. It may be a pause between the actions of God.

Eventually, each of us is going to do the same thing Jesus Christ did: die, and rise again! In the meantime, our job as Christians is to glorify God, to live in a way that reflects God's glory. It's the way we live our lives that makes God's presence known. God's glory is revealed in what we do and what we say, we who follow Jesus, we who accept His mission.

Embrace the Trinity

John 3:16-18

Most of us, as children, learned the sign of the cross - an action that reminds us of the three persons in one God - the Trinity. Some of us were shown the triangle as an attempt to explain the Trinity. Many of us were told about St. Patrick using the shamrock with its three leaves to try and explain the Trinity.

The fact is, the Trinity is a mystery, a mystery we cannot fully understand. The Father, Son, and Holy Spirit always were, always are, and always will be!

St. Catherine of Sienna said of the Holy Trinity, "You are a mystery as deep as the sea; the more I search, the more I find, and the more I find, the more I search for you."

God as Trinity - Our minds are just not large enough for us to grasp it; but here's the good news…

Even though the Trinity cannot be fully understood, it can be lived and appreciated! Our actions toward God, like prayer and the sacraments, and God's actions towards us, like God's revelations to us, help us embrace the Trinity! We come to "know" the Trinity!

God is Father: the creator who made all things and keeps them in existence. He created us and the world we live in, and gave us dominion over it! God calls us to take good *care* of His creation.

God is Son: as we read in John's gospel, "God so loved the world that He gave His only Son…" - Jesus, who set the example for our lives; and we get to receive Him in Communion! And we become what we eat, the very body of Christ on earth! What greater love could God have for us than to give us His Son?

God is Holy Spirit: the love between the Father and the Son is expressed in the Holy Spirit, the third person of the Trinity. This indwelling Spirit of God, this expression of God's boundless love, calls us to live as brothers and

Deacon Anthony C. Bonacci   *37*

sisters, to become one body in Christ. The gifts of the Holy Spirit (wisdom, understanding, counsel, piety, fortitude, knowledge, and fear of the Lord) give us the courage and strength to deal with life's every day challenges. They give us the power to overcome obstacles and transform our lives!

It's true - the Holy Trinity is a mystery. It's a mystery we accept on Faith; it's a mystery we are called to embrace; it's a mystery we can and do live every day! Let us reflect on the Father, the Son, and the Holy Spirit; let us live as thankful children of God; let us embrace the Trinity.

The Guest is Christ

Matt.10:37-42

"Hospitality"- Hospitality means receiving and entertaining guests and even strangers with kindness. In Matthew's gospel, Jesus spells out the radical commitment of being a Christian: putting Him first; giving of ourselves, and being hospitable to all, even the smallest and the simplest. He encourages us to welcome even strangers and to offer "a cup of cold water" to the "little ones."

The Catholics of Austria like to say: "The guest is Christ." In other words, hospitality to others is hospitality to Christ. The late Cardinal Joseph Bernardin told the story of his nephew Joe visiting with him. He said his young nephew's presence changed his schedule, and changed the sounds and atmosphere of his home. Hosting his nephew involved sacrifice and understanding, he said, but also brought many unexpected rewards. "Whenever we extend hospitality to others, we give something of ourselves - our time, our attention. But we also receive something in return - the gift of the persons we welcome, the gift of their uniqueness, their presence in our lives..." It's true, when we welcome and serve others, we ourselves are fed. When we "lose" ourselves in service to others, we find ourselves.

Hospitality is more than politeness or kindness. It's being present, really present to others (looking them straight in the eye). Hospitality is being present for others, even when it's not convenient. Sometimes, Christ comes at the most inconvenient times.

Sometimes, hospitality can become highly personal. Some of us need to open our lives to those who have become strangers to us: estranged family members, for example, or alienated friends; someone we've hurt or offended, or someone who has hurt us. Maybe someone we know just needs a place to rest, someone to listen, someone they can talk to in confidence.

It's not easy (we're so busy! - we have our own problems and distractions). But with effort and compassion, we can open our lives, nourish, encourage, and offer "a cup of cold water;" we can let someone know we care.

Sometimes, Christ comes in those closest to us.

Being hospitable to others can be a challenge! Discipleship is a radical commitment! You and I are challenged to put Christ first. You and I are challenged to see Christ, to find Christ in others. Saint Benedict said, "All guests should be welcomed as Christ." The guest IS Christ!

Look at the people around you; look at the "guests" who walk into your life, look at the strangers in need, look at the estranged relatives, look at the former friends... is Christ there, asking for hospitality?

Hospitality is the easiest way to get a glimpse of Christ. It's the simplest way to practice the presence of God. Whenever you or I extend ourselves in hospitality, we meet the Lord Himself; we know God in our lives; we know the reward of God's presence.

Welcome Christ as your Guest!

Come to Me

Matt. 11:25-30

Sometimes we get discouraged with the burdens of life. Dinah Shore, a famous singer of decades ago, once said, "Trouble is a part of life. If you don't share it, you don't give the person who loves you a chance to love you enough." But we hesitate to share our burdens with others, don't we? Maybe because we think, "They have enough troubles of their own."

In Matthew's gospel, Jesus calls us to trust in Him; to trust and rest in Him. *"Come to Me, all you who labor and are burdened..."* It's a warm invitation to embrace Him in trust and love, without fear. He says, "I am gentle and humble of heart."

Often, when we have a burden, we go to a best friend, a "confidant;" or maybe we go to a counselor, and that's ok (that may help); but only then, do we think to go to the Lord. Yet the Psalms tell us that He is "... our refuge and our strength." (A refuge is a place of safety from danger or trouble.) Psalm 46 tells us that even when a *nation* is in turmoil (sound familiar?), the Lord is with us. He is our stronghold!

"Come to me, all you who labor and are burdened..." In the 7th chapter of Matthew, Jesus tells us who will enter the kingdom of heaven: "...only the one who does the will of the Father..." There's the challenge! The will of the Father is that we come to Him first; permit Him into our life; share with Him our burden. He promises rest: now, from the trials and tribulations of everyday life, and later, eternal rest in heaven.

He tells us to take His yoke upon us, that His yoke is "easy." But a yoke is a kind of heavy harness; it burdens the shoulders; how can His yoke be "easy?" Here's how: When we are yoked with Him, any burden placed upon us is borne also by Him. He shares the yoke and takes the lead.

Jesus invites us to draw back from the fray of the world and allow ourselves to be healed; to come as children to the gentle One who will ease our burdens and refresh our spirits. He invites us to examine our lifestyle and reflect; to put His teachings into practice; to try on His yoke and test it; to adopt His lifestyle and see how it makes for a lighter burden – a lighter burden in the short run, and happiness in the long run.

At every Mass, we can hear in our hearts His invitation: "Come to Me, all you who are weary and find life burdensome, and I will refresh you." At every Mass, He makes Himself visible: on the crucifix; in His Word; in His ministers, in other Christians, and most of all, in the Eucharist! We come to Jesus because He is gentle and humble of heart. In Him our souls find rest, for His yoke is easy and His burden is light.

Eucharistic Unity

John 6:51-58

At work, I liked to take a walk at lunch time. Near a bakery, I could smell the warm, fresh bread coming out of the ovens. That same friendly smell that came from my Mom's oven when we came inside on a cold day; it was the promise of a great meal.

The simple sharing of bread, the simple sharing of a meal, brings about a certain unity. In our work life or in our personal life, when we want to discuss things, we say, "Let's have lunch," or "Let's have dinner together, and talk it over." We're saying, let's meet on common ground, let's come to unity.

Every church year, we celebrate the feast of "The Body and Blood of Christ." We celebrate the greatest meal that we could share, the Eucharist. We celebrate the meal that unites us to Christ and unites us to one another.

We strive to have family meals together - to foster family unity. God knows, we need strong families; families that can deal with a society that is against the family – a society of violence, moral decay, and materialism.

We gather in church as a family, a family of faith - to hear the Word, to receive the Eucharist, to be united to God and united to one another. There's a special unity there. There's love and fellowship; there's caring and sharing. Before and after Mass, we offer a listening ear; we offer loving support to one another; we are united in Christ, we share Christ with one another.

Saint Paul says, "Because the loaf of bread is one, we, though many, are one body, for we all partake of the one loaf." I once read in our parish "Prayers Answered" book, "Lord, thank you for friends and family to support us and show us YOU!" It's true, each of us and all of us are the Body of Christ!

Deacon Anthony C. Bonacci   *43*

The Eucharist is a miracle of unity. Just think - at any one time, millions of people around the world are sharing it with us.

The Eucharist nourishes our body. It gives special sustenance; it gives strength and peace, especially to the sick and dying.

The Eucharist nourishes our spirit. It gives us courage to face every day struggles; it gives us hope to make it through disappointments; it gives us reassurance when we're discouraged.

So what's the catch? What's the cost? The cost is a commitment! The Eucharist commits us to share, to share ourselves with others; to share the joys and the crosses that life deals out; to be one, united Christian family.

The Eucharist is a mystery and a miracle. The presence of Jesus in the form of bread and wine is a great mystery. The miracle is that Jesus becomes part of our very being, living in us. Jesus unites us with Himself and unites us with one another. He is the food for our journey.

The Kingdom of God

We are living in challenging times: increasing crime and violence, various addictions, abortion and euthanasia, political divisiveness, a volatile economy, Catholic dioceses going bankrupt, and the Covid pandemic! At the same time, we're dealing with personal issues: health, financial, and marital issues, the passing of loved ones.

Then we go to church, and we hear about "The Kingdom of God." You might say, "Where is this 'Kingdom of God?' I don't see it! I don't feel it. I don't even know what it is, or who it is, or when it's supposed to happen!"

"The Kingdom of God:" Some time ago, I visited our oldest daughter and her family in Washington State. Early each morning, my little granddaughter went out with me for morning exercise. Every time I tried to walk fast or jog, she saw things to stop and admire. A cat, who slowly came over and wanted to be stroked...a duck and her babies on a pond... some wild raspberries waiting to be picked...a leaf plucked from a tree. She said, "Look, grandpa, isn't it beautiful?" A child experiences the kingdom. A child sees God's presence in everyday things. Isn't that what we seek? - A glimpse of the incredible presence of God?

"The Kingdom of God:" Matthew's gospel teaches us about the slow appearance of the kingdom. Like the tiny mustard seed, the kingdom has small beginnings. Like the leaven, it slowly permeates us.

Jesus never really defines the kingdom, does He? He just tells stories about it. His stories seem to say that the kingdom is not really a place; it's more like a time. His stories suggest that we can be within the kingdom right here and now. It seems to be a process, and yet it's an endpoint (it's something to strive for).

So where is this Kingdom of God? What is this Kingdom of God? The Kingdom of God is within us. It's a way of being. It has to do with

Deacon Anthony C. Bonacci

trusting God to run things and judge things. It has to do with patience and tolerance - like the tolerance God has with us. God sees us striving to grow. That's our reason for being on this earth, to grow toward God, to develop more and more the Spirit of God within us. But God values our freedom; God waits for us to become part of His kingdom.

How do we become part of His kingdom? By applauding our children and grandchildren for their sense of wonder; maybe even imitating them; by being patient and tolerant, with ourselves and with others; by leaving judgment to God alone; by acts of faithfulness (prayer, worship, helping the poor, comforting the lonely and the bereaved, speaking out in defense of life, being informed about what happening in our beloved Catholic Church) - these things GROW God's kingdom!

The "Kingdom of God:" The Kingdom of God is within us. It's a way of being. It's a way of acting! It has to do with trust, patience, and tolerance. This imperfect world is a mixed bag of good and evil. But evil fades, evil fails in the presence of goodness. Jesus tells us to let the weeds and the wheat grow together. Let God do the final sifting!

God wants us to be part of the gathered harvest. In the meantime, His invitation to the Eucharist is a sign, a powerful sign of His patience and tolerance with us. Let us thank God for His patience and mercy, and let us embrace God's kingdom.

Who Do You Say That I Am?

Thousands of books have been written about Jesus. So many books, so many views. We, too, have many different "views" of Jesus. Some of us, on hearing the name "Jesus," think of the baby in the manger; some of us think of Him as a youngster, working in his father's carpentry shop; or as the itinerant preacher or miracle worker. Maybe we think of Jesus on the cross; or Jesus resurrected in all His glory. We may think of Jesus as best friend, or close brother. And: We may think of Jesus alive: now, today, in the Word, in the Sacraments, in His ministers, and in other people.

None of these images of Jesus is wrong, because Jesus is all these, and more. In the gospel of Matthew, He asks, "Who do You say that I am?" Peter, spokesman for the group, says, "You are the Christ, the Son of the living God." He's saying, "You are the Messiah, the One we've been waiting for!" Peter professes the true identity of Christ.

The main point is that Jesus is the Christ. All of us believe this, believe that He is the Son of the living God, or we wouldn't go to church. That's good, but what happens when we leave church? Are we witness to who He is? Do we honor His name? Do we honor His presence? Do we acknowledge His help? How do we profess our faith in Jesus, anyway? Isn't going to church enough? Of course not. Don't be a punch in, punch out, "give me my host and let me go home," Catholic!

You and I need to think about who Jesus is to us. If I think of Him as Son of God, how's my prayer life with Him? If I think of Him as brother or best friend, what have I done for my brothers and sisters lately? Am I present for others? If I appreciate Him in the Word, have I looked into learning more about the Word? If I hunger for Him in sacrament, have I made an effort to receive Him more often? Who do I say that He is? – on a personal level? Am I committed to follow Him, to live by His teachings, and obey His commandments? Who do I say that He is?

Do I use His name as a curse, or as an expression of surprise or disgust? Am I embarrassed to bow my head in public and thank Him for my meal? Do we as a family acknowledge His presence in our home? Do I attribute my blessings to "my hard work" or "luck" or "fate" or "Karma?" Who do I say that He is?

More important than the words we pray or sing in church, is the life we lead during the week; more important than the emotions we feel in church, are the motives that drive us after we leave church.

Every day, Jesus asks us where our center really is. He asks us to think about and re-commit to who Jesus is to me. He's not just someone we learn about. Christianity is about a relationship. It's true! For us as believers, the Jesus of History is the Christ of Faith. Every day, we are called to make a profound profession of faith, like Peter did. We need it, and our world needs it.

Forgiveness Without Limit

Matt.18:21-35

Why are we so reluctant to forgive others, yet we so easily expect to be forgiven by others? Maybe, it's easier to stay angry, easier to hold a grudge? The book of Sirach tells us, "Forgive your neighbor's injustice; then when you pray, your own sins will be forgiven." In the gospel of Matthew, Jesus tells the parable about the King forgiving his servant of a huge debt, and that servant being unforgiving of another servant for a much smaller debt. It's clear from the parable that we are to forgive because we have been forgiven ourselves; because we have received forgiveness from God!

"But you don't know what that so-and-so did to me!" you might say. Maybe not, but Jesus' idea of forgiveness is forgiveness without limits, forgiveness without conditions. Jesus' idea of forgiveness is accepting and affirming the other person, as distinct from their actions. Why? - Because we're all sinners; there's no perfect person.

Forgiveness does not mean we approve of the offenses that have occurred. Often, it just means we're learning to tolerate the weaknesses of our brothers and sisters, weaknesses just like ours.

When we don't forgive others, we become bitter and hard. Would you believe that studies have shown that holding grudges or a vengeful attitude are primary root causes of depression; and physically, grudges and hatred can eat us up inside.

On the other hand, when we forgive someone, we set them free, and we are set free. Forgiveness helps us to be happier and healthier; forgiveness liberates us; forgiveness helps us to grow spiritually, because it makes us more God-like.

Always remember this: To forgive is the highest and most beautiful form of love. Forgiveness brings peace, and peace brings happiness.

Like the king in the parable, God has so forgiven us. God expects us to forgive others; it's God's way.

At the next opportunity, forgive someone; and do it joyfully. At the next opportunity, ask forgiveness from someone you've offended, maybe someone you're "on the outs" with. Settle your mind and your heart; restore peace in your relationships. As a child of God, be an example of His forgiveness.

Real Christians ACT

In the gospel of Matthew, Jesus tells a story of two sons. One son says "no" to his father, but then later acts according to his father's wishes; the other son says "yes" but doesn't act at all.

Sometimes, we're like those two sons:

- sometimes, we're like the first son: we say, "no" (we sin), then later we repent, turn back toward God, and act according to the Father's will;

- sometimes, we're like the second son: we say, "Yes, Father," but we don't act; we don't follow through – because "We're too busy," or, "That costs money!" or because we're angry with that person: "He (she) doesn't deserve it." Mostly, we don't act because it's inconvenient.

Jesus tells us that real Christians act: Like the man who washes the widow's windows; or the couple who drove to Alaska not for vacation, but to build a one-room shelter for a 70 yr. old lady, hauling the wood and shingles on top of their old car; or the breast Cancer survivor with a chronically ill husband, who donates her time for the "Christ-child Society," assisting new Moms with their baby's needs; or the middle aged man who takes the bus 2-3 days/wk. to go into the inner city to help at a shelter; or the 72-yr. old lady who volunteers in a soup kitchen.

Actions speak louder than words. Acts of kindness, sharing of our time and talents are more than just words. Action is what Christianity is all about. Jesus taught us to go the extra mile to prove our discipleship. Pope Francis once said, "It's not about us! It's about selfless giving of ourselves for others!"

And the Lord doesn't ask us to succeed in every action! Any successes are His gift to us. A failed try is not the same as a failure to try. Jesus asks us to try, to strive, and when we fail, to begin again. He's always there: to listen, to help, to speak to us.

Here's the point: We can't be Christians only in our words. We are the Body of Christ. We are the hands, feet, and lips of Jesus Christ! It's the service we offer, the actions that proclaim our love for God.

Which son loved his father? The one who took action. the one who went out into the vineyard. We are called into the vineyard to do for one another!

We are called to act - to ACT like a Christian.

God Gives Us Choices

Every day, at home, at work, at school, we have choices - how many choices do you think we make in a day? Choices are nothing new. Since ancient times, God has given us choices, even in our relationship with Him. Jesus' parable in Matthew helps us understand God's relationship with us. God's story becomes our story. God is the "owner of the vineyard," the Earth He created. He gives the "tenant farmers" (His people) choices - to accept or reject the "servants," the messengers, the prophets He sends them. In the story, the people choose to reject them, even eliminate them. They even choose to reject His beloved Son.

Can you believe it? God's people chose to reject Jesus. Maybe, they didn't recognize Him? Maybe we don't recognize Him today?

And what's this about the "fruit" God expects from His vineyard? – namely, keeping God's laws and doing good works? Sometimes, people choose not to give God the "fruit" He expects.

Yet God continues to give us choices. Every day, He invites us to accept His Son, He invites us to produce good fruit.

At a fund-raiser for a local soup kitchen, they gave a used "meal ticket" to each person. They said, "[This card] contains the fingerprints of Christ Himself, Christ Himself who daily comes to us!"

I'll never forget the first time I went to that soup kitchen. The fellow parishioner who took me there stood behind the serving counter with us and as they opened the doors to let the clients in, she exclaimed with a big smile, "Here comes Jesus!"

It's true, God constantly sends His Son to us:

-not only in the hungry stranger, but in the homeless refugee; in the person standing at the end of the freeway ramp; in the non-English speaking immigrant; in the despised prisoner; in the lonely homebound person or elderly relative in the nursing home - and we choose to accept Him or reject Him;

-He sends His Son in a sympathetic spouse, in a trusted friend, in a troubled co-worker - and we choose to accept Him or reject Him;

-He sends His Son to us in the neighbor we don't like - and we choose to accept Him or reject Him;

-God sends His Son in the special needs child or in the defenseless child in the womb - and our society chooses to accept Him or reject Him. (Think about that when you vote.)

He sends us His Son in the Word; in His minister; in the Eucharist we receive - and we choose to accept Him or reject Him.

Jesus' parable challenges us to receive God's messengers, to hear them, and to heed them; to see Christ in others, and to accept Him; to choose opportunities for holiness.

"Holiness" - It's been said that "Holiness is intimate contact with Jesus."

Jesus' parable ends with these words: *"The kingdom of God will be... given to a people that will produce its fruit."*

We are called to make the right choices. We are called to keep God's laws; to do good works; to choose to produce good fruit in God's vineyard!

We Are God's Instruments

Matt.22:15-21

There's a great story in the Old Testament about God and Moses. In Exodus Chapter 4, God "uses" Moses to show His presence and power.

In the 45th Chapter of Isaiah, God "uses" Cyrus, a pagan King, to free the Israelites. The point is, God uses people to achieve His plan.

In our day, God uses us (you and me) to achieve His plan. We are God's instruments. If we are open to God, we will hear God say (like He said to Moses), *"What is that in your hand?"* If we're at home – it may be a little one, the arm of an elderly parent, a laundry basket, or a lawn mower. If we're at work, it may be a tool, a document that affects others, or an article we make. If we're at school, it may be a text or a laptop. If we're at the store, it may be a shopping cart or money. In all these places, God is asking us, *"Are you serving as my instrument? In what you're doing, in what you're saying, or in what you're using? Are you showing your love for Me and for others?"*

These are moments of grace. These are moments when God reveals Himself to us in simple everyday situations. God reveals who we are (creatures made in God's image); what we are (instruments of God's plan); and why we are here (we are here to be called back to God Himself.

The interesting thing is that God does not force us. God waits for us to come to Him. God looks for service freely given.

In our parishes, we have lectors, Extraordinary Ministers of the Eucharist, servers, and sacristans who assist at Mass. Others freely serve God's people as choir members, ushers, religion teachers, or Knights of Columbus. Some are parish committee members, volunteer maintenance persons, distributors of food, clothing, and household needs, or volunteers at the local food pantry. There are couples who work with Marriage Encounter, Cum Christo, & Kairos ministries. Our clergy give of themselves; all is "service freely given." All are people who make time for God, people who "give to God what is God's," as Jesus said. These are people open and willing to be God's instruments. As St. Paul says, "We give thanks to God always for all of you."

Bishop Desmond Tutu, once said, "...we do not need to prove ourselves to [God]. We do not need to impress God, for God's love has taken the initiative..." So, if God doesn't force us, and if we don't need to prove ourselves to God, if God will love us anyway, why should we do these things? Why should we strive to be God's instruments? - To pay our debts to God; in thanksgiving for God's many blessings.

Maybe we don't think of ourselves as God's "instruments." Maybe for some of us, God and religion is an external thing, something we do on Sundays, or on special occasions like baptisms, weddings and funerals. Maybe we've blocked God out with our pride, or our selfishness, or our indifference, or our fear. Maybe we need to think about that.

An American Baptist pastor, recently quoted in the Catholic Digest, said, "God has taken vessels just like you and me - marred and flawed as we are - and used us in great and mighty ways." Sooner or later, we come to realize that God uses our strong points and our weak points to move us forward, to achieve His plan. Sooner or later, we are willing and eager to be His instrument.

Today and every day we are called. May we respond to God, "Yes, Lord, make me your instrument."

True Greatness

Matt. 23:1-12

What is "True Greatness?" Have there been any truly great persons in your life? One I knew was a farm boy from Kansas; a boy who worked his way through school, all the way to a Ph.D. degree, becoming a full Professor and Associate Dean of his college. This man led the prayer of invocation at every college function. He was a humble man who would say, "Just call me Jack" when people would address him as "Dr." or "Dean."

In Matthew's gospel, Jesus challenges the status-seeking and hypocrisy of some of the Scribes and Pharisees. (Remember, the "Scribes" were interpreters and teachers of the Jewish Law, and the "Pharisees" were the religious leaders who professed to be observers of that Law.) Jesus urges the people to follow their teachings, but he cautions them to avoid their hypocrisy. They preach one thing and practice another. Jesus exposes their desire for titles and seats of honor, and their love of self-display, e.g., the use of phylacteries and tassels.

Jesus' words are a warning for us. We can be the Pharisees of our day. We can take titles too seriously, we can covet places of honor. We can be living our faith sincerely, but falling into hypocrisy. We need to be careful that our lives match our words. We need to get closer to true greatness and closer to real humility.

Real humility is not putting ourselves down, nor denying our achievements. In Jesus' view, real humility is acknowledging our worth as human beings, our dignity as Children of God. Real humility is pride coated with gratitude. It's sharing credit for our achievements with God and with others…

Maybe you know a truly great person. When you praise them for an achievement or honor, they say, "Yes, God's been good to me," or, "Thank you, I am truly blessed." Real greatness is acknowledging the presence of God and others in our achievements.

In this gospel, Jesus tells us to avoid status-seeking. He tells us to humbly serve others. He says, "The greatest among you must be your servant." This is true greatness.

When my colleague "Jack" passed on a several years ago, a Jewish colleague spoke of Jack's greatness, his avoidance of status-seeking, and his service to others. He said, "The thing I most admired about Jack was that Jack didn't wear his Christianity on his lapel like a pin; He lived it!"

The challenge for us is to *live* our Christianity!

Christt in Our Midst

Matt.25:31-46

"…whatever you did for one of the least brothers of mine, you did for Me."

At a local soup kitchen or food pantry, one meets clients with various backgrounds and various degrees of neediness; and one meets local volunteers reaching out to help them.

In Matthew's gospel, Jesus identifies with "the least" - the hungry, the thirsty, the homeless, the sick, and the imprisoned. He tells us that He is in our midst. He asks us to minister to Him.

Where do we start? When is there time? (We have jobs, children, homes to maintain, shopping, cleaning, cooking, games, plays, concerts, practices…)

How about this: once a week, we can reach out to a neighbor, or a co-worker, or someone at school, or a stranger, who is hurting or lonely or sick or in mourning; maybe just a phone call, or a card, or a short visit, or a listening ear. We can get involved a little; we can offer a kind word, a ray of hope; we can reach out to Christ in our midst.

That's the point! Loving service to those in need is service given to Christ Himself. And here's the best part: loving service to those in need is a way to experience Christ in our midst (something we all want). Jesus isn't "back then." Jesus is alive, here and now, in the Word, in the Eucharist, in His ministers, and in other people.

We should ask ourselves, "How does Jesus Christ want me to minister to Him? Who is He in my life?"

In these tough times, we are re-discovering What really matters in this world: FAITH, FAMILY, FRIENDS, and HELPING ONE ANOTHER - And this is exactly what we need to carry on. Experiencing Christ in our midst gives us the power, and the strength, and the grace to carry on.

As one bishop said to a group of Confirmandi, "The first time Jesus came, He came as a babe; will we recognize Him when He comes again? Learn to recognize Him in the faces of those in need."

Are You Ready?

Matt.25:1-13

A popular song on Christian radio says: *"So people get ready, Jesus is coming. Soon we'll be going home. People get ready, Jesus is coming to take from the world His own."* But that's just a doomsday outlook, isn't it?

On the other hand, studies show that we had 3 times as many natural disasters in the 90's as in the 60's. Lately, we've had record numbers of tropical storms, hurricanes, wildfires, floods and earthquakes.

But that's just a big coincidence, isn't it? The late Pope John Paul II once said, "In the designs of Providence, there are no mere coincidences."

This gospel from Matthew focuses on readiness: It's a gospel about Jesus' coming. It asks us, "Are you ready?"

At the end of each church year, the readings have "apocalyptic" images, i.e., images that reveal God's plan. The liturgies are "eschatological," i.e., liturgies that relate to the end times. The Church gives us time to think about death; time to think about the end of the world; and time to think about our own readiness. As Jesus said, *"[We know] neither the day nor the hour."*

Are you ready? If He doesn't come sooner, the Lord will come at the moment of our death. You might say, "Yeah, I know, but hey, there's no hurry; heaven can wait!" It's natural to fear death; it's natural to cling to life. But for each one of us, our own death will mark the end of this world. Some of us will have time to prepare, some won't. Sometimes, a person is told months or years ahead that their death is imminent.

I've had more than one terminally ill person tell me, "You know, I'm really lucky!" "Lucky?" "Yes, I have time to prepare, time to make peace with God and others, time to get ready." But some people are caught off guard, called suddenly by violence or an accident.

Are you ready? Ask yourself, "Do I frequent the sacraments? Do I try to keep God's commandments? How do I treat others? Do I pray every day?

Deacon Anthony C. Bonacci 61

When I put my head down on that pillow every night, do I say a good act of contrition? Can I honestly say, like Jesus did, *Father, into your hands I commend my spirit?*"

The end seems far off. Maybe it is, and maybe it isn't. Whether it's our own death or the end of the world - the point is not so much when; the point is the wisdom of readiness.

Matthew tells us that the deepest wisdom, the fullest readiness is living chastely, living honestly, living nonviolently [Matt.5], and meeting our neighbors' basic needs. The book of Micah says, "...act justly, love mercy, and walk humbly with your God." [Micah 6:8].

So be wise while we wait. In the meantime, be alert for the signs of His second coming, and be prepared for the possibility of His calling us home first. Frequent the sacraments; study His Word; be nourished by His Body and Blood; hear in the Mass the priest pray, "...as we wait the blessed hope and the coming of our Savior Jesus Christ!..." Grasp this promise, grasp this promise as comfort! And BE READY; be ready to meet the Lord when He comes OR when He calls!

Cycle B Reflections
(Based on Sunday Gospels for Cycle B)

"Show me O Lord, Your Way"

(Psalm 27:11)

Mary – Our Mother and Our Model

Luke 1:26-38

As children, many of us learned about Mary. We learned that Mary is our mother, and Mary is our model. We learned prayers and hymns to the Blessed Mother, and we learned to pray the rosary.

In the gospel of Luke, we read the story of the Annunciation, when the angel Gabriel tells Mary that she will be the mother of Jesus. Mary humbly accepts her role as Mother. With total faith and trust, she says "Yes" to God.

Mary is *our* Mother, too. Like all good mothers, she is always there to rejoice with us in the happy times and listen to us and comfort us in the sad times.

Mary is our model. She accepts even what she can't understand. Every day, we are asked to accept things we can't understand: losses, illnesses, the passing of loved ones, broken relationships. It's difficult to accept what we can't understand. We want to understand! We want to know what God is doing in our lives. (*"Why now, God?; Why me, God?"*)

All the while, Mary models for us a simple, abiding faith, *"I am the handmaid of the Lord. May it be done to me according to your word."*

Gabriel's message to Mary is for us, too: like Mary, we are blessed; like Mary, we need not fear; like Mary, the Lord is with us.

Mary is God's masterpiece. She is "mother;" she is "model." She lights the way and leads us to God. The challenge for us is to imitate Mary as we go to her in prayer, giving ourselves totally to God and trying always to do God's will.

As children, many of us learned the beautiful prayer we call the *"Memorare":*

"Remember, O most gracious Virgin Mary, that never was it known that anyone who fled to thy protection, implored thy help, or sought thy intercession, was left unaided. Inspired by this confidence, we fly unto thee, O virgin of virgins, our mother. To thee do we come, before thee we stand, sinful and sorrowful. O mother of the Word incarnate, despise not our petitions, but hear and answer us. Amen."

Angles

Are angels real? The Bible says they're real. Church Tradition and Church Councils say they're real. The Catechism of the Catholic Church says angels are "spiritual beings without bodies, servants of God, created by God to carry out God's missions" as messengers, or as guardians.

A poet once wrote:

> *"Angels, 'tis but seldom they appear,*
> *So neither do they make long stay;*
> *They do but visit, and away..."*

The word "angel" comes from the Greek "angelos," meaning "messenger." We hear about angels hundreds of times in the scriptures: Gabriel, who brought Mary the invitation to be the mother of the Messiah; the angel who appears to the shepherds and proclaims the good news of Jesus' birth; the angel who appears to Joseph in a dream and tells him to take his family and flee to Egypt; the angels who ministered to Jesus in the dessert and who strengthened Him in His agony in the garden; the angel who on Easter morning rolled back the stone to the tomb and announced the Lord's Resurrection; the angel who released the imprisoned apostles; and the angel who instructed Philip to take a particular road.

Angels are messengers. They bring us good news, they open our eyes to moments of wonder or to special people, to the idea that God is here in our midst! The book of Revelation tells us that an angel presents to God the prayers of Christians on Earth.

Angels minister to us. They sit silently with us when we mourn and they console us and offer us healing and hope in times of suffering and doubt. They help us through the storms of life.

Angels protect us. They warn us of danger and guide us and lead us to Jesus. The *Catechism of the Catholic Church* says, *"Beside every believer stands an angel as protector and shepherd,"* and Psalm 91 says, *"...God commands the angels to guard you in all your ways..."* At every funeral, we say, "...May the angels lead you into Paradise..."

Angels don't get much attention today, probably because science can't prove their existence. Your belief and my belief in angels is based on Sacred Scripture, the Tradition and teachings of the Church, and our own experiences. Angels are part of God's creation gift to each one of us.

May we thank God for His Angels! May they guide us and guard us always!

A Holy Family

Luke 2:41-52

In elementary school, the good Sisters and teachers taught many of us what a "holy family" should be:

- a family that worshipped and prayed together;

- a husband and wife in a loving relationship;

- children who were obedient to their parents and grandparents, aunts and uncles, and other adults in authority;

- family members who were loving and loyal to one another, especially in times of troubles or suffering, or when the small family business was in trouble.

In the gospel of Luke, we get a hint of the love and bonding in the Holy Family of Jesus, Mary, and Joseph. Jesus *"... went down with them and came to Nazareth, and was obedient to them; and His mother kept all these things in her heart. And Jesus advanced in wisdom and age and favor before God and man."* So what is a "holy family" today?

Families are so different today. There are so many kinds of families: some are traditional families; some are "empty nesters;" some are extended families, with grandma or another relative living with them; some are "blended" families; some are single parent families; some are single persons taking care of a relative; and some are single persons living alone.

Today, there are so many hindrances and obstacles to being a "holy family:" including the influence of social media, broadcast media, and the internet. But in spite of the fact that we live in different kinds of families today, and in spite of the fact that this is a different world today than it was in Jesus' time, or when we grew up, we can still imitate that first "Holy Family."

St. Paul suggests Christian virtues to "put on," like putting on our overcoat, virtues that help us to be "holy families:" kindness & forgiveness, gentleness, compassion, humility, patience, thankfulness, and LOVE as the bond - the "glue" holding it all together. LOVE is the bond of family life!

St. Paul admits how difficult we can be to each other. He says, "*bear with one another.*" We all have our idiosyncrasies, our peculiar sensitivities, moods, likes and dislikes. We are challenged to accept the other person, and not try to force them into being something they're not. We are to take into account the other person's limitations, pressures, fears, and the burdens they may be carrying.

On a higher level, all families are part of a larger family, God's "Holy Family." Whether we're a traditional family, or a special kind of family, whatever the size or configuration, each person and each family has a place important to God. Each family, is a little "Church." As we love & care, give & share, within our own family and among families, we minister to each other and we sanctify God's family. We make it holy.

Jesus Calls Us to Imitate Him

Mark 1: 29-39

In Mark's gospel, Jesus commands an unclean spirit to come out of a man. Then He visits Simon's house, grasps the hand of Simon's mother-in-law, and her fever leaves her, and she's well enough to serve them.

After dinner, the people bring others who are sick. He heals them, driving out demons, but the people, even His followers, misunderstand Him - they think He's some sort of magician! They want to make a "show" of Him, but He wants no fame. He wants them to see for themselves who He really is. He wants them to know that He was sent by the Father.

Jesus is setting an example for the people and setting an example for us. He's calling us to imitate Him: healing, serving, praying, and evangelizing.

First, we are called to heal one another. When you or I touch or embrace someone as an expression of sympathy; When you or I offer words of compassion for someone's illness or surgery; When we lift up the spirits of a spouse or child who has had a hard day, or a school friend or co-worker who suffers a disappointment - we are healing. We are imitating Christ!

Second, we are called to serve one another. Sometimes we wonder why good people suffer. But often, this is God's call for someone to serve. I will never forget a former student and colleague, a talented professional man in his thirties who was slowly dying of a terminal illness. His sister left a successful career on the West coast to come to Central Ohio to be with her brother, to serve for over two years as his daily care-giver. She renounced her "rights" and "privileges" for the sake of someone else - her sick brother. Contrary to the "culture of death," she chose to serve her brother.

When we serve the needs of an ill or frail loved one; when we visit the lonely or the sick; when we attend a funeral; when we feed or clothe the hungry and homeless - we answer God's call to serve. We imitate Christ!

Third, we are called to pray. Jesus often went off "to a deserted area" to seek communion with the Father. Do we "retreat" or "withdraw" from our busy world to pray? If we can't physically retreat due to the demands of our job or family, we can mentally retreat, taking a few minutes for prayer first thing in the morning or at bedtime. Jesus sets the example. He asks us to imitate Him.

Fourth, we are called to evangelize. Some people travel to missionary lands, some knock on doors, and some carry "Jesus" signs around at football games. Maybe that's not our style, but we could share one of God's little miracles with a friend or co-worker, perhaps a real life experience when we felt God's presence (one of those "God-incidents"). We could invite an inactive Catholic or a school friend to church with us, perhaps someone who tells us they're going through a tough time. This is evangelization!

We could ask ourselves: "How can I heal others; how can I serve others; how is my prayer life; how can I evangelize?"

Every time we receive the Eucharist, we unite in the Body of Christ, and we are called to something grand – we are called to imitate Jesus: healing, serving, praying, and evangelizing.

Healing and Being Healed

Mark 1:40-45

I once represented my parish at a "Community Support Group" of educators, administrators, church representatives, city and civic leaders, fire, police, and medical health professionals who came together to support the students, parents, teachers, and residents of our school district as we mourned the terrible tragedy of suicides of two of our young students.

We came together to begin the healing of our community. All told, the effort was to reach out in love and compassion to our students, parents, families, and teachers during a difficult time; the group effort was to heal and be healed.

In Mark's gospel, in a very personal encounter, Jesus heals a leper. The leper seems very humble and believing: *"If you wish…"* he says to Jesus. He seems very trusting and confident; he seems to know that Jesus can heal him. Jesus is sensitive, gentle, and compassionate: *"I do will it…"* He says.

Today, very few people have "Hansen's disease" (leprosy). But we do have "lepers" in our society: social outcasts, outsiders, and strangers we put on the fringe: the homeless, the unemployed, and the poor; the "frail elderly," the handicapped, and the prisoners; the addicts, the immigrants, and persons of other races, cultures, and nationalities; the depressed, the mentally ill, and the mentally challenged. These are just some of the "outsiders" in our lives.

When Jesus touched the leper, that contact made Jesus ritually "unclean…" But Jesus touches him anyway. Why? Because the man was "on the fringe;" precisely because he was excluded from the community. Jesus transgresses ritual law when a human need calls for it. For Jesus, the person was more important than any category or label. Jesus' actions were always in service of the great commandment: love of God and love of neighbor. Jesus made it clear that charity is higher than any law.

We need to ask ourselves, "Are we willing reach out when a human need calls for it? Are we willing to "touch" the needy stranger out of love of God?" Sometimes, it's not easy to reach out in love - because it's not convenient, or because it's not popular.

Jesus wanted to change the attitude toward the "lepers" of His time. He wants to change our attitude toward the "lepers" in our lives. We are challenged to reach out and "heal" the outsiders in our lives: those who need our love, our compassion, and our healing "touch."

Jesus is the great healer; but in this world, we are His touch. We are His hands, His feet, and His lips. We are His instruments, and the best part is, we meet Him in those we serve!

Ashes and Perspective

Every day, life gives us experiences that help us keep things in perspective. My cold or sore throat is insignificant compared to someone who is hospitalized. My burnt toast is a tiny nuisance compared to a famine in a third-world country. My annoyance with other drivers is petty compared to a distant nation at war.

I once knew a wealthy, influential person who died suddenly at a relatively young age. This was a man who owned thousands of acres of land, and who was the founder and chairman of the board of a large business. A few years later, a poor and unknown farm hand who worked for the rich man also died. To this day, when I walk in the cemetery where they are buried, I pray for both of them, and I reflect: There they lie, within a few steps of one another, and I think of the words we use on Ash Wednesday: *"...unto dust you shall return."*

The ashes we receive on Ash Wednesday are really "dust." Ashes help us keep things in perspective. Since the earliest Jewish rituals, they represent mortality; we receive them as a remembrance of our mortality.

For many years, I worked with a very devout Jewish man. When we were going through busy and stressful times, I would get consumed with trying to get everything done. This wise man always helped me keep things in perspective. I can see him shaking his bent finger at me and saying, "God forbid, you and I be run down by a truck tomorrow. But if that happened, this place would keep right on going. No one is indispensable. Our families would miss us, but they would go on; life would go on, without us...." I never forgot that insightful comment, and it has helped me to keep things in perspective.

To keep things in perspective, we could ask ourselves some sobering questions:

>Where am I going in life?
>
>What am I doing with my time?
>
>What priorities do I live by?
>
>What changes should I make?
>
>What should I be more serious about?; Less serious about?
>
>Do I get angry or lose sleep over little things?
>
>Do I need to push myself more on worthwhile projects?
>
>Do I need to slow down and give more time to my family?

If we think in terms of ashes, it puts these things in perspective. It's a good and joyful thing to encounter God's mercy and God's love. Pope Emeritus Benedict once said, "Mercy is God's promise, and love is God's business."

Desert to Dessert

Mark 1:12-15

In Mark's gospel, we read of Jesus being alone in the desert and being tempted by Satan, just as we are tempted. He overcame the test and angels ministered to him.

Temptation is a form of suffering. We know that Satan will tempt us, just as he tempted Jesus. Satan's business is to frustrate the work of God, to insert an uncertainty between us and God. Satan's never happier than when he's pulling us apart from each other: husband from wife, parent from child, brother from sister, friend from friend. Satan's never happier than when he's pulling us from Christ.

But here's the good news: just as there are evil forces in this world, there are good forces. God does not abandon us. When we think we're at our lowest, that's when He's the closest. We have angels, too – it may be our spouse, a brother or sister, a special friend, a teacher, a grandma or grandpa, or even a stranger.

Here's a little secret: we have to be OPEN to God to recognize the angels; open to God to receive the strength to overcome the temptations; and open to God to be able to withstand the sufferings. That's when He's the closest. That's when we recognize Jesus' presence. Openness to God is one of the most effective forms of prayer.

When we think of desert, we think of dryness, suffering, even death; when we think of dessert, we think of sweetness, the promise of something to come, and life.

There are times when we have to walk through the desert. These are times when we should open ourselves to God and recognize God's presence. These are times to minister to ourselves and to others. These are times to contemplate the dessert, the Resurrection, and the reward to come.

Deacon Anthony C. Bonacci

We are the Temple

John 2: 13-22

What if you were asked, "Where do you find God?"   Some   might say, "In Church; in the Eucharist; in the Word; in Nature…"

Some years ago, on a business trip, I found God in Boston. There, I met a man named "Ed," a regional Manager for a large drug company. We were having dinner after we set up for a seminar, and as we got to know each other, we talked about our families and shared some pictures. Ed said, "You know, I really look forward to taking my family to church on Sunday. When I go to church with my wife and kids, it transcends everything else. It goes above and beyond my company, my job, my possessions, my worries. I really look forward to prayer and fellowship with other Christians... to the nourishment I receive from the Eucharist and from the Word."

This man had zeal for God's house, for God's temple. He showed eagerness to be in God's house. His witness to me and his sincere sharing from his heart, showed me that he himself was a "temple of God."

St. Paul writes, "*You are the temple of God, …the Spirit of God dwells in you. The temple of God, which you are, is holy.*"

We are the temple! Individually, and collectively, we are "Church," the Body of Christ in the world today; the temple where the Spirit of God dwells.

God is in our midst when we comfort, support, and encourage one another and when we forgive one another. God is in our midst when we witness to one another. God is in our midst when we teach (and even admonish) one another. Our Christian words and actions demonstrate that we are the temple.

Our Christian words and actions are so needed today - today, when our society seems to have no respect for life; when abortion and euthanasia are legal; when we witness violence and terrorism, even in our churches and

Reflections for Everyday Life

in our schools; when we have legal, "recreational" drug use; when violence permeates TV, movies, and even video games. This is the culture we are living in.

The challenge for us is to turn this culture around, one temple, one person at a time, one family at a time, one congregation at a time. As individuals, we could start by looking at the Word, where God delivers the commandments. We could ponder them (even one) mentally when we start our day, or when we go to bed at night.

In our family, we could talk with our children and grandchildren about the things they see in our culture, the violence and social injustice in the world. We could explain how these things are contrary to our Christian beliefs - in the sacredness of life, the sacredness of marriage, and the sacredness of the body. Thus, as our family matures physically and spiritually, we build up God's temple.

In our parish congregation, we build up God's temple when we gather to worship. This gathering is special, a gathering that is holy. In that sacred space, we celebrate the presence of God. We talk to God, we listen to God, and we tell God about our joys and sorrows. We praise God and we thank God. We ask for God's help and God's forgiveness. In that sacred space, in His temple, God reveals His presence - in the Eucharist, in the Word, in His ministers, and in His people. When we leave that place, God's spirit flows out from each of us, from each person, from each family, and from our congregation.

Always remember St. Paul's words, *"You are the temple of God...the Spirit of God dwells in you...the temple of God, which you are, is holy."*

The Cross is Triumphant

John 3: 13-17

Philip. 2:6-11

When you look at a cross, what do you think about?   Perhaps we see the broken, bloody body of Jesus as gruesome or even repulsive. Perhaps we feel sad or sympathetic, as we think about Jesus' humiliation, and how he subjected Himself to this.   Or we may feel deeply moved, emotionally stirred, as we think, "Even though Jesus was God, He laid aside His glory (He "emptied Himself"), to save us, to save me.

Sometimes we come to church feeling physically or emotionally broken, and as we gaze upon the cross, we ask "Why, Jesus? Why the cross? Why my cross? Dear God, give me the strength to carry on!"

Sometimes we gaze upon the cross and feel God's love, or a peace, a calmness, the answer to a prayer.

We wear crosses on necklaces and lapel pins, and we carry crosses in our pockets, or on our rosaries. The cross is the most visible sign of our Christian faith, but how often do we think about the deeper meaning of the cross? How often do we see it as a symbol of victory and life?

In His dialogue with Nicodemus, Jesus teaches the triumph of the cross. He tells Nicodemus that the Son of Man must be lifted up for our salvation, for our eternal life. He implies the healing power of the cross, as He recalls the healing power of the rod and serpent raised by Moses in the desert.

As Christians, we are called to be with Jesus; we are called to bear the "crosses" of everyday life: as children, struggling with homework, grades; as teens, the strong feelings of independence, conflicts with parents, the challenges of a new relationship and career concerns; as adults, the stresses of married or single life, family, children, jobs, and finances; in middle age, caring for aging parents, high school and college children; as "Senior

Citizens," loneliness, frequent illnesses, the loss of a spouse and/or life-long friends.

Regardless of our age, our sufferings and disappointments are a sharing in the cross of Christ. They're part of being a Christian. They remind us of our need for God. Mother Theresa once said, "If He suffered for love of us, then we can suffer for Him, it's a connection!"

The good news is that Jesus lives with us on every cross. He helps us, guides us, and sooner or later, He shows us their purpose, their meaning. Through our crosses, He brings us closer to Him and to others.

We may know someone who has had an accident or health problem, but as a result of that situation, has a new circle of friends, or has adopted a better, healthier life style, or has simply re-arranged their priorities in life.

We may know someone who has gone through a difficult job change, but find out, in time, that they're better suited to the new job, or discover a new talent they never knew they had, or maybe have more time for family.

Perhaps there's been a serious illness or a death in our family, a heavy cross for everyone, but as a result, we draw closer together, and there's a certain peace or even a reconciliation between some family members who never got along.

Just as Jesus' cross is triumphant, our crosses can be triumphant. Just as Jesus' cross represents healing, our crosses can represent healing. Just as His cross shows God's love for us, our crosses can show our love for God. And when we open our arms in love and support to others carrying their crosses, His cross is again triumphant, again healing.

In his second letter to the Corinthians, St. Paul says,

"We are afflicted in every way possible, but are not crushed; full of doubts, we never despair. We are persecuted, but never abandoned; we are struck down but never destroyed."

The challenge for us is to offer everything we experience in the spirit of the cross. Then we can carry on with confidence; then we can call on the triumphant Christ to strengthen us, to heal us, and to give us hope.

As we gaze upon the cross, recognizing the victory of Christ, we claim the healing power of Christ. He triumphed through that cross; we will triumph through that cross.

Deacon Anthony C. Bonacci   79

Jesus is the Greatest Teacher
John 12:20-33

In John's gospel, Jesus tells us what awaits Him and what awaits us as we move on toward another life. He sounds hopeful, He sounds purposeful, and He sounds committed. Eternal salvation for all mankind will be the "fruit" of His death.

In His early ministry, Jesus calls us to heal, to serve, to pray, and to evangelize. In this gospel, the teacher Jesus models obedience for us. He demonstrates how to accept God's will; He guides us to prayer; and He motivates us to glorify God. But are we paying attention to the teacher?

We often cry out in times of trouble: couples struggling with marriage problems, moms and dads agonizing over family problems, or people dealing with employment problems or the pains of relocation and separation from loved ones.

It's not easy to surrender to God. It wasn't easy for Jesus, either. Sometimes we forget that He experienced the human condition fully. Even as He's teaching, He admits His human weakness, and hints of His fear of death. He says, *"My soul is troubled now, yet what should I say- Father, save me from this hour? But it was for this that I came to this hour..."* Then, in spite of His human weakness, He denies Himself, and accepts the Father's will. He turns to the Father with faith and hope, and says, *"Glorify Your name [through me]."*

The Father, who enabled Him to endure the cross, will strengthen us, too, if we turn to Him with faith and hope, if we commit our lives to His care. We strive to be good students of the Great Teacher. We want to learn and understand His teachings; we want to discern God's will. We want faith and hope in times of trial, and the strength, power, and grace needed for everyday life. We want to glorify God's name by our actions, like Jesus did.

When we celebrate the Eucharist, we can make a commitment to a deeper knowledge of God, and a practical recognition of God in every action and situation.

Faith is a Way of Life

John 20:19-31

There seems to be a certain order to believing: doubt, struggle, faith, and awe. In John's gospel, we read the story of Thomas' doubt. Thomas said he needed to "see" and "touch" the wounds of Jesus. Thomas wanted to believe, and was probably struggling to believe. A week later, he's there when Jesus comes. He's had time to work through his doubts and struggles, and he makes the most profound and complete expression of faith in all the gospels: "MY LORD AND MY GOD!"   Thomas was in awe of the resurrected Christ.

Sometimes we have doubts, even doubts about our faith. But our doubts can be an occasion for stronger faith. When doubts of faith occur, we can *exercise* our faith. We can work through our doubts. We can study and read about our faith; we can consult the catechism or other books; we can talk with our clergy; we can pray. Doubt can be the occasion for a *stronger* faith. It may involve a struggle, but life is full of struggles.

Some years ago when I was a teen-ager, we were sitting around the kitchen table (our little "church" at home), and we were asking our parents about "faith." My Dad, who was a man of simple but great faith, said, "You know, kids, how sometimes when Mom or I hear some startling news about someone in the family or about something that happens in the world, how we blurt out, 'MY GOD!' We don't do that to take God's name in vain. No, it's a natural reaction. We have doubts, we don't understand why God allows some things to happen; we're struggling, we're reaching out to God for His help. Faith is a bridge between us and God. Faith is giving ourselves, trusting ourselves to God and trying to do what God wants us to do."

About forty years later, Pope John Paul II said, "Faith ....is giving oneself totally to God and striving always to do God's will..." He added,

"Faith is not just intellectually believing..." In other words, faith is not just "head stuff." It's not just accepting a set of religious beliefs.

Real faith is a way of life. Real faith is freedom from the need to reason everything out. Real faith is not needing to "see" everything or even understand everything.

The challenge for us is to develop ourselves as people of faith, to work through our doubts and struggles, and to use this "faith" way of life as our "bridge" to God. When faith becomes our way of life, we find ourselves in awe of God - in awe of God's signs, wonders, and everyday miracles. We become "faith people."

Jesus calls faith people "blessed," blessed because they don't have to "see" and "touch" in order to believe. Through doubt, struggle, faith, and awe, God is with us all along, calling us to oneness with Him, calling us to a loving relationship with Him.

Hang in There!

John 10:11-18

We often ask, "How's it going?" or "How are things?" Often, the other person says, "Oh, I'm hanging in there..." But sometimes, we detect a little worry or sadness, or even a little boredom. Is it worth it to "hang in there?"

Jesus, the Good Shepherd says, "Yes!" He proves it by sharing His life with us, His resurrected life. For example, when He heals us or restores us - that feeling you get when you know the medicine is working. Is it the medicine? A health professional would say, "Yes, it's the medicine." A believer would say, "But who gifted the person who discovered that medicine?"

Recall that feeling you get when a friend or family member picks you up when you're feeling down, or offers an encouraging word when you're worried. Who sent that person into your life at just the right time?

Jesus, The Good Shepherd shares His life with us when He makes us "Children of God," not only at our Baptism, but in our lives today, and in the life to come. St. John verifies it: he says, *We are God's children!* He's saying, "We are adopted sons and daughters of God, we are brothers or sisters to Jesus!"

Those "Precious Moments" statues that we see on wedding cakes or on greeting cards are successful because they capture how precious we are in God's eyes.

Jesus, the Good Shepherd shares His life with us when we claim the gift of salvation and when we trust in His promise of eternal life. We can't even imagine what's in store for us in heaven: the ecstasy of being in God's presence where there is no pain, no sorrow, no troubles, and no disease.

If one of our deceased loved ones could speak to us today they would say, "Springtime is only a tiny taste of the joy to come; you think that full moon, that star, that comet, that space station floating overhead was beautiful? You should see it from here; it's only a speck in God's universe!"

They would say, "IT IS WORTH IT TO HANG IN THERE, because the Resurrection is real; The Resurrection is the source of new life!"

Jesus, the Good Shepherd, laid down His life for His sheep, for you and for me, to heal and restore us, to make us Children of God, and to gift us with salvation.

We are gathered into one flock. We are destined for heaven, and in the meantime, Jesus feeds us with His Body and His Blood, the Eucharist. Jesus, the Good Shepherd makes the Resurrection real in our lives. It is worth it to "hang in there," because the best is yet to come!

Expressing God's Love

John 15:9-17

Love expresses itself in many ways. In the gospel of John, Jesus says, "As the Father loves me, so I also love you."

The Father's love comes first. Love originates in the Father.

The Son loves us as friends. He wants complete joy for us, and He tells us how to achieve that joy - by obedience to God's commandments, and by loving one another.

We love one another out of affection for God, because we are His sons and daughters. As we grow in love, we aren't happy with small-talk love, we aren't happy with pat-on-the-head love. We want to get involved, we want to do something about it. We may not have to give our life like Jesus did, but make no mistake, love calls for action. We are called as spouses, as parents, as children, as friends, even as strangers, to sacrifice for one another.

God's love expresses itself in many ways. Often, it's the little things, like giving a few minutes of attention to someone who really needs it right now, when it's inconvenient.

St. Ignatius says, "Pay attention to the gifts of God in your life; that will give you gratitude, and that will help you pass on God's love to those who most need it."

Perhaps you are feeling unloved; perhaps you are feeling unlovable. Remember John's words: "God is love." Remember Peter's words: "God shows no partiality..." Above all, remember Jesus' words: "As the Father loves me, so I also love you..."

Love originates in the Father and comes to us through the Son. We are called to reciprocate that love by obeying God's commandments and by loving one another. We are called to recognize God's love, to accept God's love, and to share that love with one another.

Whenever we give or receive love, God is present!

New Life

Mark 2:18-22

Think about the major changes in your life and how it affected you: perhaps marriage: dedication to another person and their welfare (real love); or the birth of a baby, and the attention to its needs first, before all else; or a new job and relocation, a new boss, new people, and new equipment; or entering high school or college with new ways of learning and new kinds of tests; or separation or divorce or the loss of a spouse, being single again.

Can you continue to do things the "old way?" There's a new way of doing things, a new way of living. The old ways are not appropriate anymore; they don't work anymore. This happens in our spiritual lives, too. Sometimes, the old ways don't work anymore.

In this passage from Mark, Jesus offers an image of Himself as a bridegroom, a spouse present for us. What an image - Jesus is saying, "I am the groom, celebrate with Me! Embrace Me!" It's like celebrating with a new bride and groom, overflowing with love.

In the parables of the cloth patch and the wineskins, Jesus is saying, "I offer you a new life in Me, in My Way of doing things!" But for you and me, this new life requires a new attitude, new ways of doing things; we can't just plod along the old way. We can't do the minimum just to get by; we can't live by society's standards all week long, and relegate God to Sundays, nice and neat in a "Sunday compartment."

All week long, society says, "Chastity for singles, faithfulness for marrieds? - that's old fashioned; integrity in government? - that's good for a comedy skit; honesty in business? - that's outdated! safety in schools? - you'd better get yourself a gun!"

One psychologist jokingly said, "Yeah, that's right, folks, say anything, do anything, as long as it feels good; go ahead, cheat or lie, get even, just make sure you get what you want!"

As Christian believers, we believe in "new wineskins" - *actions* we take to embrace Him, the "new wine;" actions like making everything we do a "prayer" (even our work); actions like changing rude or abusive behavior (the way we talk to family, or the kids at school, or the people at work); actions like forgoing something we really like to eat or drink, as a way to say "We're sorry, God;" actions like donating money or time to a good cause. Prayer, fasting, and almsgiving - sounds like the Sermon on Mount, doesn't it?

At every Eucharist, we celebrate the groom's presence with us. Jesus says, "*I offer a new life... embrace Me! I am 'the new wine' ... you can't put Me in old skins.*"

The challenge for us is to embrace this new life in Christ through new ways of Christian living and new ways of Christian actions. We shoud live with the same joyful hope that Mark held out for those first Christians.

The Storms of Life

Mark 4:35-41

In the gospel of Mark, Jesus speaks to the apostles in the midst of a storm and tells them they should not fear. Then to prove it, He orders the storm to stop.

We've all been through storms: natural storms like drenching rain or snowy blizzards or hail and wind storms, maybe even a tornado. It's scary; it's not easy to weather the storms, but storms bring out the best in people. Most of the time, storms bring us closer to each other; storms bring us closer to God.

We all struggle through the storms of daily life: Sometimes, it's a stormy relationship (with spouse, or a parent, or a child); it may be a storm at work (with the boss or a co-worker); or it's the storm of a serious illness or accident; or the sudden passing of a loved one.

All these storms challenge our faith. Sometimes, it seems like everything is falling apart. The stress and worry may be more than we can bear. We may turn to heaven, pleading with God, "Where are you, God? Don't you care?" (like the apostles in the boat, waking Jesus, "Lord, do you not care that we are perishing?!")

Jesus' response: "Quiet, be still!" He commands the wind and the sea, He commands a calm in the storm; He asserts His power; He demonstrates His Divinity. Jesus shows the apostles (and us) that He will always be there, not just for nature's storms, but in all the storms of our lives. God never abandons us. Jesus slept in the back of the boat during the storm because He had complete confidence in God the Father.

God will protect us through the storms of life. God wants to free us from our fears. In every Mass, after the Our Father, the priest prays, "Deliver us, Lord, from every evil and grant us peace in our day. In your mercy keep us free from sin and protect us from all anxiety..." It's an expression of our Faith, and here's a secret: the deeper our Faith, the deeper will be our peace. Recall how many times, after we get through a personal trial, even the passing of a loved one, how we feel a deeper peace, a deeper serenity, a deeper closeness to God.

We will sail through many storms in our lives. But Jesus' words and Jesus' actions are both challenging and consoling: He challenges us to be patient in the face of storms, stresses, and anxieties. He consoles us to not be afraid; and to never, never despair. And to help us, God has given us the Body of Christ (our fellow parishioners) to love us and support us, day after day, week after week, around His holy table. As we offer the gifts, as we offer ourselves, as we receive the Eucharist, Jesus whispers, "Be not afraid of the storm! I am always with you!"

Rest in Him

"Come away by yourselves ...and rest a while."

Jesus wants us to rest in Him. That's easier to say than do. Some years ago, as a young professional with a family and career, I discovered it was difficult to find a balance between work and rest. Even today, when I try to "rest," I start thinking about what I was supposed to do, or what I need to do.

In this gospel, Jesus is moved with compassion when He sees the crowd "...like sheep without a shepherd." He is moved with compassion when He sees us, sometimes feeling deserted, lonely, unsure - like sheep without a shepherd.

"Rest in Him." Shepherds nurture and protect. Jesus shepherds His exhausted disciples to a private place for rest. He shepherds us in our private places, because He knows that we need a sense of direction.

Sheep are vulnerable creatures and can be easily hurt. They're defenseless against predators and need a shepherd to lead them and keep them safe. You and I are vulnerable creatures. Sometimes we feel like lost sheep, confused, unsure, and hurt. For example, when a friend lets us down or betrays us. We like to present ourselves as self-assured and self-directed, but something like that can break our hearts.

So where shall we turn? Our consolation and our encouragement comes from our Shepherd – the true Shepherd – Jesus. He is always there, no matter where life takes us, no matter the trials and tribulations we encounter. He loves us and cares for us.

Sometimes He's ahead, leading, perhaps when we're invited to join a Bible study, or teach Sunday School. Sometimes, He's behind, pushing, perhaps when we hesitate to "get involved," but have that nagging feeling that "I should be doing something!"   Sometimes, He's along side, accompanying us, in times of loneliness, or in quiet times, or when we're trying to figure out how to overcome obstacles. And often times, He carries us, like when a loved one passes, or when there's a job loss, or a serious illness or accident.

It's not easy! It takes a lively faith; we need to be actively involved with the Shepherd. We need a deep, living relationship with Him. We have to reach out to Him, like He's our brother, which He is. We have to communicate with Him, intimately. We have to talk with Him, as we would with a close friend, sharing our life with Him, speaking from our heart about our deepest concerns, and telling Him we trust Him as our shepherd. Only then can we "rest in Him."

St. Augustine said, "O Lord, our hearts are restless until they rest in You." The more personally we relate to our Lord, the deeper our friendship, and the more we lose the feeling of being "sheep without a shepherd." Jesus wants us to "Rest in Him."

Sharing the Nourishment

John 6:1-15

When I was a boy, my Mom and my aunts made various home-made breads in different shapes and textures. I fondly recall the smell and taste of that warm, fresh bread, so delicious and so nourishing.

Whenever they served a new loaf, they first took the bread, gave thanks (making the sign of the cross on the bottom of the loaf), and only then cut it and serve it to us. When we asked, "Mom, why do you do that?" they would say, "We are thanking God that we have this bread to eat." To this day, my siblings and I still carry on this custom.

Bread – a simple nourishment Jesus feeds to the crowd. Jesus takes barley loaves from a little boy willing to share what he had, gives thanks, breaks them, and gives them to the hungry crowd.

When we hear this story, we probably wonder - what really happened here? What was the real miracle, anyway? Was there a real "multiplication" of the loaves and fishes right before their eyes? Maybe. John calls Jesus' miracles "signs" - signs to show the people who Jesus really was - the Son of God.

Some scholars say this story is a lesson in the power of sharing. Maybe it was Jesus' willingness to share the few loaves and fishes that encouraged others to share what they had, and so everyone ate; maybe that's the miracle.

In any case, Jesus uses the loaves and fishes to show us who He is, and to show us that He wants us to offer ourselves - not just our food - but our gifts, our time, our talents - and let Him take them, bless them, break them, and share them with those in need. Jesus invites us to imitate Him; to reach out and meet the needs of others. This is the Body of Christ at work!

Jesus says, "I am the bread of life." And so He is. He nourishes us with the Eucharist (food that nourishes our body and our spirit); He nourishes us with His Word (Scriptures and homily that feed us for the week as we make decisions, face struggles, and relish joys); He nourishes us with each other (family, friends, colleagues, neighbors we share our lives with). The challenge is to allow ourselves to be "broken," to be "poured out" in service to others, to extend ourselves, to make sacrifices, even to be inconvenienced for others.

Jesus feeds the hungry crowd - that's us! This meal is a real miracle. It's a miracle of people sharing; it's a miracle of unity and love. We gather at Mass to receive Christ; we gather to be Christ to others; we gather to share the nourishment!

Integrity vs. Hypocrisy

Mark 7: 1-8, 14-15, 21-23

In the gospel of Mark, Jesus uses powerful words against the Pharisees. He calls them hypocrites, because they set aside God's laws in favor of human customs. They are more concerned about clean hands than clean hearts. Jesus' is saying, "You two-faced phonies!" He knew they had hate (even His murder) in their hearts.

Might He be talking to us?

Certainly we're not hypocrites, Lord? We have a nice church, a nice altar, and statues, candles, and flowers; and we sing and say prayers, and receive communion, and even shake everyone's hand at the sign of peace. But what we do here doesn't always show what's really in our hearts, does it, Lord? You say it's what's inside that counts. When we walk out of church, do we act with faith; do we offer hope; do we show love?

Surely, we're not hypocrites, Lord? We tell our youngsters not to lie or swear, or cheat, or drink, or smoke. We tell our teens to drive courteously; but sometimes, we don't practice what we preach, do we, Lord? We tell our spouses we love them; we tell our teachers and bosses we did our best; but sometimes our actions don't match our words, do they, Lord?

And Your commandments - those "shalt nots?" Well, sometimes, we just have to go along with other people, you know, Lord? Sometimes, it's just more comfortable to not speak up, to go along with the crowd; I have to "save face," you know? I have to "cool."

Come to think of it, Lord, our whole society is hypocritical nowadays. We pour millions of dollars into high tech equipment and treatments to preserve and prolong life, but we allow the murder of babies in the womb, even the dissection and sale of their parts; and we allow millions of OUR tax money to go to the largest abortion provider in the country.

God, give us the courage to speak up and speak out to our civil leaders and STOP this barbaric atrocity!

Moses said, "Hear God's laws and observe them carefully...don't add or subtract from them..." He advises us to *cherish* God's laws. They're not just a bunch of "shalt nots." They're blessings from God that guide us.

James tells us to "Welcome the word that has been planted in you...be doers of the Word..." In other words, act according to the word of God. Care for those in need. Live by values other than the world's values.

Jesus calls us back to basics - to put God's laws ahead of our customs or our comfort; ahead of our desires, our habits, or even society's so-called "choices." Jesus calls us to be persons of integrity - to make our actions match our words. Jesus calls us to be pure of heart - to respond to God from within; it's what's inside that counts. As a little boy once said, "Holiness is when you're clean on the inside."

Obstacles to Discipleship

Mark 10: 17-30

What's an "obstacle?" It's something that stands in the way. In the gospel of Mark, Jesus says that things (possessions) can be an obstacle to following Him. The rich man says to Jesus, "I follow the commandments..." but he has an obstacle to following Jesus (all his stuff).

What's a "disciple?" It's one who follows another, one who believes and spreads the teachings of another. Jesus asks us to be His disciples, to follow Him.

What's a "commitment?" It's an agreement or promise to do something in the future. Jesus asks us to make a commitment to Him, to trust Him and only Him.

Obstacles to being a disciple are not just things. Jesus is talking about *anything* or *anyone* that prevents us from being His disciples, from being committed to Him.

We could ask ourselves, "What's my obstacle? What holds me back from following God's call? Maybe it is "stuff." Things or money can give us a false sense of security; they can pull us away from God; they can separate us from family, friends, or our faith. For example, siblings fighting over "stuff" or money when parents pass on.

Maybe it's work: Many of us would probably admit that at some time or other in our life, we've let work become our God.

Maybe it's the people we associate with, or the places where we spend our free time - do they help our faith life, or do they weaken it?

Maybe it's sports or hobbies. Sports and hobbies are good, but how about when they become an obsession, i.e., taking priority over our worship time? "Sorry, Father, that swim meet, that soccer game, that practice, is on Sunday, and we have to be there, you know?"

The media - TV, Movies, and the Internet – can be good diversions, but sometimes, they compromise and ridicule our beliefs. TV shows and movies often mock religion, portraying it as "quaint" or irrelevant or portray clergy as out-of-date dummies. We have a secular press that puts their "spin" on the news – mis-interpreting what the Church stands for and why, often providing mis-information or dis-information.

Personal traits can be obstacles. For example, selfishness ("It has to be my way, or I'll pout, I'll give you the silent treatment."); or gossip or ridicule (putting others down to make myself look good).

Sometimes, we hide our obstacles: "Nobody at work or at church will ever know." But the book of Hebrews says there is no hiding from God; God sees completely.

Jesus challenges us to remove the obstacles, to let go of the things or relationships that separate us from Him; to commit to Him, and to be His disciple.

But that's not all, because then Jesus says, "You can expect persecutions." We might ask Him, "Lord, are You asking us to obey the commandments, to share with the poor, to remove the obstacles, to follow You as a disciple and commit totally to You, and then expect persecutions, too?

And our Lord says, "Yes; I know what it's like; I was a human once, remember? Look at the cross, and see what they did to me!"

Discipleship is not easy! Being a Christian is a combination of promise (eternal life) and persecution (guaranteed). It's a combination of blessings and sufferings. But our fellowship with God and others grows in the process.

Each time we receive the Eucharist, we commit to removing our obstacles; we commit to becoming His disciple.

Humble Servants

Mark 10:35-45

We have all known servants in our lives – some famous, some not so famous. I once knew "Jack," a poor farm boy from Kansas who worked his way to a Ph.D. degree, and who became a professor, researcher, and Associate Dean of a health care college.   As a teacher, advisor, and mentor, he insisted to students and colleagues, "Just call me Jack." He saw himself as a servant to others.

Some of us have been servants or caregivers for a parent, spouse, child, or friend who can no longer care for themselves. We humbly as needed.

St. Martin dePorres served the sick poor of Lima, Peru, including unwanted infants and children. He came to be known as "Martin the charitable," another humble servant of God.

Oscar Romero, archbishop of El Salvador and a champion of social justice was murdered on March 24, 1980 while giving a homily. He was canonized in 2018. Mother Theresa, servant to the poorest of the poor in India, is also now a saint of the church.

Of course, the greatest servant of all was Jesus Christ, who stooped down and washed the feet of the disciples, telling them that He was "giving them an example…as I have done, so you must do…"

The gospels tell us what it really takes to be a disciple of Christ. Again and again, Jesus tells us that the role of a disciple is *service*. He tells us to follow the commandments, to take up our cross, and to be of service to others. That's what qualifies us as a disciple of Christ!

In the gospel of Mark, Jesus challenges James and John, who are jockeying for position next to Jesus. He exposes their ambition for the "seats of honor." Jesus makes it clear that our status in society is irrelevant to being a disciple.

He says, "Can you drink the cup that I drink…?" He's asking them (and us), "Can you join your suffering to mine? Can you offer up the trials and tribulations of every day life? Can you join them to my suffering on the cross? - And still be of service to others?

Jesus says, "Blest will you be" if you give yourself in humble service to others. Every night, as you rest your head on the pillow, ask yourself, "Have I tried to serve God today? How can I serve God? Am I willing to serve humbly?

You may ask, "What's the reward?" Most often, the reward is simply realizing that in helping others, we give them HOPE, and in doing so, we help ourselves become more Christ-like, and that's what it's all about – becoming more Christ-like.

When my former colleague "Jack" passed on, a Jewish colleague honored Jack's humility and service to others. He said, "The thing I most admired about Jack was that Jack didn't wear his Christianity on his lapel like a pin; He lived it!"

The challenge for us is to live our Christianity as humble servants. That is practical and pure Christianity!

Your Faith Will Save You

Mark 10:46-52

Has your faith ever saved you?

When we think of "faith," we think of "trust," we think of "belief;" we may think of the familiar phrase, "Letting go, and letting God; letting the Lord take over."

The *Catechism of the Catholic Church* says Faith is "Man's response to God."

Our late Holy Father St. John Paul II said, real Faith is "Giving oneself totally to God, and striving always to do God's will."

In the Cursillo movement, we talk about "Grace" and we talk about "Faith." *Grace* is God's gracious gift of Himself to us; God's unconditional love, unmerited and unearned; God calling us to a loving relationship.

The thing is, we can either accept or reject God's help. We can accept or reject God's grace. It's our choice! God makes the offer, but God doesn't force us. God awaits our response. Here's the point we make: a faithful Christian accepts God's help, accepts God's grace. *Faith* is our response to God's grace. Faith is a person's acceptance of God's plan. It's our response to God. Again, St. John Paul's definition of Faith: Faith is "giving oneself totally to God, and trying always to do God's will."

In the course of my life, my Faith has saved me many times. God's grace comes exactly when we need it: in times of struggle or suffering or doubt. Our part is to be alert, to be aware of God's offer of Himself. Our job is to respond in Faith.

I can't imagine how anyone who doesn't have Faith can handle the trials and tribulations that occur in life: the illnesses, accidents, disappointments, financial concerns, personality clashes, losses of loved ones, and all the rest that are part of life. You and I, as faithful Christians, believe that God already knows our problems. He knows that there are times we will need to lean more heavily on Him for strength and courage, for His love, and for His grace.

In John's gospel, there's a story of a man born blind. At first, the blind man refers to Jesus as "that man they call Jesus." Then he calls Him "a prophet." Then, "the Son of man," and finally "Lord." His faith develops gradually, his insight comes slowly, just like ours. The important thing to remember is that God is always there. Sometimes He's ahead, leading, like when we're invited to join a men's group or ladies group, or to teach a religion class. Sometimes, He's behind, pushing us, like when we hesitate to "get involved," but have that nagging feeling that "I should be doing something!" Sometimes, He's alongside, accompanying, in those times of loneliness, or in quiet times, or when we're trying to figure out how to overcome obstacles. Sometimes, as many of us have experienced, He carries us, like when we lose a loved one, or when there's a serious accident or illness.

The faith-filled Christian accepts God's help; the faith-filled Christian takes part in God's plan!

Preparing for the End

Mark 13: 24-32

In the Fall, we tend to think about "endings:" the end of the calendar year and the end of the church year.

In November, 1999, everyone was worried about "Y2K." People were preparing for "The End." Rumors were flying: "We might lose our computers, our electricity, and our heat; we might have no oil, no gasoline, no water, no food!" People were preparing for "The End." They stocked up, even hoarded everything: fuel, water, and food; people bought generators, preparing for what might happen. Some said it might be the end of the world. People were prepared for the end… or were they?

In the gospel of Mark, we have an image of the "end times." Maybe this image is not to be taken literally, but it is to be taken seriously. We might say, "I'm too busy to worry about the end of the world;" (or) "When it comes, it comes. I just hope I'm not here when it happens." Some of us might think, "Am I ready? How do I prepare for the end?"

Jesus tells us that only God the Father knows the future. He tells us that no person, not even He, the Son of God, knows the day, or the hour when the End will come. Jesus' real message is about personal preparing. He tells us to be watchful; He calls us to be alert.

How do we prepare - personally? By being "prophetic." This is not about predicting the future. Being "prophetic" is watching out, being alert for signs of God's presence: in everyday events and in everyday experiences. For example, when God sends an event or a person into our life that clearly *reveals* Himself to us. We've all had these experiences.

Being prophetic is being alert to the events around us: alert to their affect on us and our families. Being prophetic is being a fearless spokesperson for what's right, in our families, in our workplace, in our schools, and in our society. It's speaking out against the genocide in our country – abortion! – it's speaking out against the non-negotiables of our Catholic faith: euthanasia, fetal stem cell research, and cloning. Theologian Walter Brueggemann says it's "nourishing a perceptive alternative to the perception of the culture."

Being prophetic is speaking out for truth, transparency, and accountability in our beloved Catholic Church.

Being prophetic is teaching our children and grandchildren about the deceptions we see in our culture, including so-called "gay marriage" and the media glorifying "alternative life styles." Then, having done our best, being prophetic is trusting in God to handle the rest, trusting in God that Truth will prevail.

This is "preparing for the end."

This reading from Mark is good news! It encourages us, it cools our fears, and it comforts us. No matter what troubles or evils we face, it gives us hope. It reassures us of God's presence, and verifies that God the Father will triumph over evil.

Then we can comfort others: family and friends who may be fearful, or indifferent, or angry with God; even those who may be despairing.

In every Mass, we hear the priest say, "…and ready to greet Him when He comes again…" and "…as we wait the blessed hope and the coming of our Savior, Jesus Christ…"

We needn't fear "The End" - not if we're prophetic. Jesus will come to judge. As Christians, we expect that. In the meantime, the challenge for us is to focus on the task at hand, to focus on being the best prepared Christian we can be. If we're personally prepared to enter the Kingdom, it doesn't matter when the end comes.

Cycle C Reflections
(Based on Sunday Gospels for Cycle C)

"Show me O Lord, Your Way"

(Psalm 27:11)

Repentance Begets Forgiveness

Luke 3:1-6

"*Repentance*" is heartfelt sorrow for offenses against God or against others, and a resolve to do better in the future. In Luke's gospel, John the Baptist calls the people of his time to repentance. Jesus' cousin John calls *us* to repentance, calls us to prepare our hearts for the coming of the Messiah.

We all know John's mission - to be Jesus' forerunner, to be God's messenger. His message is, "Repent, turn away from sin, prepare the way" for Jesus.

Consider how we prepare for a visit of someone special: we clean house, we scurry around and tidy up; we get all cleaned up, we wear something nice, and we try to look our best. That's what we're called to do spiritually. We're called to clean up and tidy up spiritually, for Someone special.

We begin with repentance. In our hearts, each of us knows our offenses against God. They're probably the same old sins, over and over: usually, our offenses against others - probably right in our own families. We could ask ourselves, "How have I offended my spouse, or my brother or sister, or my parents or my children?"   Or maybe we've offended someone at work, or at school, or at the store. We need to ask forgiveness and we need to make amends.

You might say, "But that's so difficult! I'm just too busy, anyway! Maybe I'll do it later, when Aunt Jane or cousin Fred comes to visit. Then I'll tell them how sorry I am for what I said to them last April." Now is the time to do it. Now is the time to heal old wounds, to make peace, to apologize, and to forgive.

Now is the time to look back over the current year to see if we've grown spiritually, or if we've stood still? Maybe we've back-peddled. Now is the time to be honest with ourselves; to reject society's message that nothing is sinful anymore! It's a lie! Sin is still sin! Now is the time to straighten our path, to smooth out our rough ways. Now is the time to prepare our hearts.

Remember always, we have the sacrament of Reconciliation: God offering us forgiveness for all our offenses. *Repentance begets forgiveness.*

Someone special is coming and we want to be ready. We hear the call coming through the baby's cousin, John: "Make ready the way. Remove the selfishness, remove the impatience, remove the intolerance, remove the hurtful words, let go of the hostility, remove whatever makes it difficult for the Christ child to come into your heart."

John's message is the same today as it was two thousand years ago: "Repent, forgive, change your ways, make straight your path; the Righteous One is coming." As Luke says, "The Word of God came to John." The Word of God comes to us.

What Ought We To Do?

Luke 3: 10-18
Phil. 4: 4-7

Some years ago, a simple bracelet with the letters, " W W J D" were very popular. The letters stood for "WHAT WOULD JESUS DO?" They were a reminder whenever one was trying to make a decision. Should I do this or not? Should I help that person or walk away? Should I say something, or should I be quiet? What would Jesus do (in this situation)?

In Luke's gospel, the "crowd" asks John, "What ought we to do?" These were ordinary people like us, searching for answers, looking for words of comfort; people like us, asking John, "What should I do to be ready for Jesus?" John says, "*Share...*"

Then, the tax collectors (who were known to be crooked) come up to John and ask, "What ought we to do?" Sometimes we're like the tax collectors: we find ourselves in situations where we could profit by "bending" business ethics a little, or "bending" the rules a little, or "bending" the truth a little. John says, "*Be fair...*"

Then the soldiers (who were hired guards for the Romans) ask, "What ought we to do?" Like the soldiers, sometimes we're in a situation where we can bully someone or show them disrespect - maybe it's an employee, or someone who's younger, or elderly, or smaller, or weaker; sometimes, like the soldiers, we gripe that we should have more. John says, "Respect people, don't bully them; be content with what you have."

John knew that some in the crowd needed to repent; they needed conversion. John reminds them (and us) of the judgment, not so much as a threat, but as a call to action, as good news that the judgment will affirm us if we live according to the will of God.

When we have a cross to carry, or when we're struggling with a really tough decision, we can still rejoice, because we can turn to HIM. No matter what we've done, or where our decisions have taken us, we can come home.

In his letter to the Philippians, St. Paul says, "Be kind to all." We can practice gentleness in our homes; we can be considerate to the part time sales clerk; we can show courtesy at work and on the road.

St. Paul also said, "Avoid needless worry." Psychologists say there are two kinds of worry: guilt, which is worry about the past, and anxiety, which is worry about the future. In either case, Paul has the answer to worry: An attitude of gratitude (Prayer with thanksgiving). Prayer with thanksgiving is the antidote to worry.

These words from John and Paul are a call to action. We can share, we can be fair, we can respect others and be content with what we have. We can be kind, we can avoid needless worry, we can pray with gratitude. Mother Teresa once said, "We cannot do great things on this earth; we can only do small things with great love."

God wants us to share in the love and joy of His kingdom.

The Epiphany Continues

John 2; 1-12

When I was a boy, I often visited "Aunt Jenny" & "Uncle Mike." Typical Italian immigrants, they always made homemade wine. They drank some, at meals, but mostly, they gave it away to their "paisanis," their friends. They never seemed to run out of wine. They would go down the basement with an empty bottle, and come up a few minutes later, proudly tapping the cork into a full bottle of wine. It amazed me then, and it still amazes me, to think that Aunt Jenny and Uncle Mike could change forty cases of grapes into a barrel of beautiful red wine.

In the gospel of John, Jesus changes things. He changes water into wine of the highest quality so that the wedding feast can go on. The message is, "The Messiah has arrived!"

Every year, we celebrate the "Epiphany," the manifestation of Christ: the Magi following the star, longing to see Jesus, just as we long to "see" Him in our lives.

Every year, we continue the Epiphany with the Baptism of the Lord, when Jesus was baptized by John, the Father's voice giving clear approval of His Son, just as we seek God's approval in our lives.

The story of Cana continues the Epiphany. Jesus is made more evident, more present in His first miracle. We, too, want Jesus to make Himself known in our lives.

If these three events (the Magi, the Baptism, and Cana) make up the Epiphany, does that mean the Epiphany is over? No, the Epiphany continues!

The Epiphany continues when we experience those special moments when God manifests Himself to us personally; moments when we feel

God's presence in a special way. Perhaps, when as a youngster, we received our first Holy Communion; or when as a young adult we received our Confirmation; or when we held our first baby; or when a loved one passed on. Each one of us could relate special moments when we've felt God's presence in a special way.

The Epiphany continues when we manifest God to others, when our actions and our decisions make Christ's presence evident to others. For example:

-When we teach our children or grandchildren our Faith and practice it with them;

-When we use our gifts and talents to support and encourage each other;

-When we use our gifts, our talents and our treasures to serve our parish family;

-When we challenge the culture of violence and death, and promote the sacredness of life;

-When we call for Truth, transparency, clarity, and accountability from our church hierarchy.

We need these experiences of God; we need experiences that encourage our faith to grow. We can't change water into wine, but we can work wonders with the gifts God has given us. When others see that God is alive and at work in our lives, their faith is strengthened, and they are inspired to make changes in their lives.

Just as Jesus changed things at Cana, we can change things in the world today. Just as Jesus was the visible sign of the Father, we are the visible sign of Jesus. Just as Jesus manifested the Father's presence, we manifest Jesus' presence.

We are His instruments. We continue the Epiphany.

Sinners and Hypocrites

John 8:1-11

When I was a boy, the good Sisters of Mercy taught us about sin. They taught us that each time we disobeyed God's commandments, we sinned. To help us understand sin, they said that each sin was like a "black mark" on our beautiful white soul.

Maybe that wasn't so silly, because sin is a dark stain, a dark stain in our relationship with God. Sin is an offense against God; a turning from God; a separation from God. Sin is our deliberate choice to do wrong vs. God, or against another person. We will to do it. It doesn't happen by accident.

In the gospel of John, Jesus convicts the Pharisees (the religious "show-offs") of their sin, and of their hypocrisy; their pretending to be sinless. Jesus forgives the woman caught in sin. He doesn't condone her sin, but He forgives her. His forgiveness of the woman gives us comfort. It's comforting to know that Jesus forgives, even forgives a sinner caught in the act.

During the weeks of Lent, we think about our sins and we review our lives. Maybe some of us feel that we've committed a sin that cannot be forgiven, or a sin that we're just too embarrassed to confess; or afraid to confess?

Most priests we know would tell us that there isn't a sin they haven't heard. The fact is, if we're sorry for our sins, and we confess our sins, God forgives us of our sin, any sin.

It's hard to admit our sinfulness, isn't it? In the Confiteor, we say, "I confess to almighty God and to you, my brothers and sisters, that I have sinned…" But do we mean it? Are we sincere? Or are we hypocritical – like the Pharisees?

"Hypocritical"- That's when our actions don't agree with what we say. Sometimes, we rationalize our sins, kind of "justify" them ("everyone's doing it" (wink, wink); or we play the "blame" game ("that co-worker made me do it; that wife of mine made me do it!" Many times, like the Pharisees, we overestimate our saintliness, and we underestimate our sinfulness; or we put others down to pump ourselves up. We're so conscious of others' defects but unconscious of our own. Sometimes you and I are hypocrites.

Yet God, giving us free will, allows us to choose - even to choose to sin. We decide. By the way, temptation is not a sin. Even Jesus was tempted by the devil. It's when we agree, when we choose to do wrong, that it becomes a sin.

Any time is a good time to recall our sins, and the sins we allow in our society. We could ask ourselves, "How has this day been for me, personally? Have I come to a reconciliation with God and with others? Have I experienced conversion? Am I ready to confess my sinfulness to God and others? If we're hesitant, remember this: God's love and God's mercy is infinite.

Jesus doesn't throw stones at the woman, nor at us. He doesn't will her death, nor our death as sinners. Jesus wants us to be converted and live. His infinite mercy invites us. His constant call is to conversion.

Every time we receive Him in the Eucharist, we answer His call to conversion.

Do You Love Me?

John 21:1-19

In a memorable, heart-warming scene from "Fiddler on the Roof," Tevye encounters his wife Golde with that most important question, "Do you love me?"

In the gospel of John, the Risen Jesus encounters Peter with the same important question, "Do you love Me?" Remember, Peter had *denied* Jesus three times. Now Jesus offers Peter a chance to repent by declaring his love...three times!

Every day, the Risen Jesus encounters us in opportunities that come our way; in the decisions we make; in people who cross our path; even in trials we face.... and the question is the same: "Do you love Me?"

First, we have to recognize Him. In the story, John, not Peter, recognizes Jesus. John had a special "love-vision" for Jesus. We need that kind of vision.

Every Christian knows that real love is always put to the test: whether we're married, or single, or widowed, or clergy, or a student, the Risen Jesus asks us, "Do you love Me?" And if like Peter, we say, "Yes, Lord, You know I love You," Jesus says, "Do you really love Me:

-even knowing that the Christian life is not easy? (it includes disappointments and suffering);

- even knowing that the Christian life may take you where you don't want to go?

- even if you may be inconvenienced by someone who needs you right now - someone who's lonely, or afraid, or upset, or lost?

- even knowing that you may suffer criticism for doing or saying something that's not "popular" in society?

- even if you must take a stand for life, and against violence?

And if we still say, "Yes," He says, "Follow Me...."

Deacon Anthony C. Bonacci   *115*

Maybe we're not called to be Peter, who followed Him to a real cross, but we *are* His disciples. We are called to encounter Him, recognize Him, love Him, and follow Him.

Understanding the Holy Spirit
John 14: 23-29

When we were little children, we learned to make the sign of the cross: "…and the Holy Spirit."

At our Confirmation, we learned that we receive the "Holy Spirit" and His gifts, including the gift of "understanding."

In High School & College, before tests and exams, we said the prayer: "Come Holy Spirit, fill the hearts of thy faithful…" We were asking the Holy Spirit to help us recall what we had learned, and our understanding of the Holy Spirit grew.

Our understanding of the Holy Spirit is an on-going process. As we grow and experience God in our lives, we develop a deeper understanding of "Holy Spirit."

In the gospel of John, Jesus is telling the disciples what's going to happen, and He is leaving His farewell gift, the gift of the Holy Spirit:

-the Father will come to those who love Him and will dwell with them;

-this "Paraclete" (the counselor, the comforter) will teach and remind them of all that He had told them, and will bring them a special peace. They will know that God dwells in them and guides them.

Jesus is telling *us* that this same Paraclete, this same indwelling of God, will teach us, will "re-mind" us of Jesus' words and presence, and will bring us a special peace. Jesus is telling us what's going to happen. He's giving us the awesome gift of the Holy Spirit.

We often need the Paraclete, the "helper," to remind us of Jesus' words and deeds, and to teach us what they mean in our life. We often need the "Counselor." Sometimes He comes as a fleeting idea or insight when we're not expecting it. Maybe it's the answer to a problem that's been in the back of our minds, or the answer to a prayer, and we know deep inside what action we have to take. Sometimes we feel compelled to call or visit a friend or relative who's been on our minds all day, and when we do, we find out they really needed to talk to someone. Sometimes we sense guidance for a new direction in our life. Maybe there's been a painful job change, but as we struggle through it, God's will becomes clearer.

We all have experiences like this, and we should share them, because they give witness to the Holy spirit working in our lives. They remind us of God's presence.

It's amazing how God dwells in each of us, speaks to us in a "human" voice, in our thoughts, in our prayers, in our reading, and through other people. Some people call this the "whisper" of God, or the "soft voice" of God.

We need the "Comforter" to bring us that special peace,   that "Shalom" kind of peace, especially on the days when everything seems to be breaking loose. We need to be reminded that God is in charge; that God dwells in us and guides us, no matter what happens.

We have a special connection to God the Father: the "Holy Ghost," the "Holy Spirit," the one we call "Paraclete," "Counselor," "Comforter." He continues Jesus' work; He recalls Jesus' teachings; He leads believers to all Truth.

The Holy Spirit is that Divine indwelling who reminds us of God's very presence; who reminds us of Jesus' words and deeds; who teaches us to recognize God's acting in our lives, and to recognize God's will for our lives. The Holy Spirit gives us the strength and courage to keep on going, and brings us the special peace of the risen Christ.

Revelation of the Trinity
John 16:12-15

Every year on the beautiful feast of Trinity Sunday, I recall a certain Saturday morning some years ago. It was a men's bible study, and we were talking about the Trinity (Father, Son, and Holy Spirit). One of the men reminded us that we are "created in God's image." As I headed home, I wondered, "How does this compute?" When I got home, I wrote in my bible:

God-Father (creator): like my mind, my creative part

God-Son (Incarnation):like my body, my temporary part

God-H.S. (abiding presence):like my soul, my   everlasting part

At the time, I thought, My! This is pretty good stuff! I've got this Trinity thing all figured out! Of course, I didn't have it all figured out, because none of us truly understands the Trinity. But this insight was a "revelation" for me, a moment when God made Himself known to me.

"Revelation" means how God makes Himself known to us; how God speaks to us.

In the gospel of John, Jesus says to his disciples, *"I have much more to tell you, but you cannot bear it now. But...the Spirit of truth...will guide you to all truth. [He] will declare to you the things that are coming."* Jesus is not talking about prophecies of the future, rather a clearer, fuller understanding of who He is, and His will for us.

You might ask, "What does that mean for me?" Just think, from time to time, haven't you had a special or profound insight or revelation from God? One of those special "aha" moments?

"Revelation:" Some years ago, a priest friend and I were sharing a few of those special, personal incidents when God reveals Himself to us (those "God-incidences"). My friend said, "You know, God's revelation is all around us, if we just open our eyes and ears and listen!" It's true, isn't it?

Deacon Anthony C. Bonacci   *119*

We need God's revelation in our world. We need His guidance, and we need a clearer understanding of His holy will for us. We live and work in a society where science and "high-tech" seem to be the gods; where Christian values are challenged or seen as simple-minded; where the media depict Christians as "quaint;" and where a vocal minority is trying to impose a dangerous and immoral "standard" on us and our children.

The good news is that we have that guidance we need - we have the Holy Trinity as our source of energy, strength, and courage. God is Father, God is Son, and God is Holy Spirit. We can call the Father "Abba" - "daddy" or "papa," who guides us, guards us, and protects us. We are brother or sister to the Son Jesus, who walks beside us, always. We have the Holy Spirit, the abiding presence of God, the "breath" of God, the Advocate, the Counselor, the Comforter, who helps us to say the right thing, and make the right decisions.

The secret to the mystery of the Trinity is this: As we go through life, God reveals Himself to each one of us in special ways, in different ways, and in little bits and pieces. Sometimes, God reveals Himself in a prayer (public or private); or in one of the sacraments. Often, God reveals Himself in other people (someone we know who evokes the presence of God to us). Sometimes, God reveals Himself in the Scriptures. Perhaps most often, God reveals Himself in the everyday joys and sorrows of life ("…if we just open our eyes and ears and listen").

When we accept and respond to God's revelation, those special, personal moments, we experience the life of the Trinity; we discover God acting in our lives. We come to know God as Father, Son, and Holy Spirit.

The Eucharist is the Greatest Meal

John 6:1-15

Do you remember the aroma of fresh bread from your Mom's oven? It was the promise of a great meal to come.

At our house, my Mom would turn the fresh loaf on its side, and with the tip of the knife, make the sign of the cross on the bottom of the loaf before cutting off the first piece. We asked, "Mom, why do you do that?" and she would say, "We are blessing the bread, and thanking God that we have something to eat."

As we grew up, we continued that custom, blessing each new loaf and giving thanks before slicing it and passing it out.

Bread is a simple nourishment, but it's always part of a great meal. It's like the greatest meal that we share at Mass: Christ in the Eucharist.

The meal we share is nourishment for our body and for our spirit. This special food satisfies our hunger; our hunger for Christ in us. He gives us courage to face our every day struggles. He gives us hope to make it through the valleys of disappointment. He gives us reassurance when we're discouraged. The Eucharist uplifts our spirit, and helps us to focus on God.

This meal we share is a remembrance, a memorial of Jesus' death. St. Paul says, "Every time, then, you eat this bread and drink this cup, you proclaim the death of the Lord until He comes." Every Mass, every "Liturgy of the Eucharist," is a re-living of the Last Supper and Jesus' death the next day.

This meal we share is a miracle, like the miracle of the feeding of the 5000. It's a miracle of people sharing ! It's a sign of unity and love among us. Often after Mass, people offer a listening ear, people offering loving support to one another, people share Christ with one another!

This meal we share is a promise, a foretaste of the heavenly banquet that awaits us. This greatest of all meals is nourishment, is memorial, is miracle, is promise.

What's the cost of this great meal? It's priceless, but it's free. However, there is a challenge, there is a commitment involved. This meal commits us to share in Christ's death - by offering our lives for the sake of others; bearing and sharing the crosses that life deals out; and being strong and patient when things don't always go our way....in short, by being a Christian!

In the feeding of the five thousand, Jesus nourishes His people. He takes the barley loaves from a little boy willing to share what he had. He gives thanks, He breaks the loaves, and He gives them to the hungry crowd.

Jesus still feeds the hungry crowd - that's us! As the Psalmist says, "The Lord feeds us; He answers all our needs." He feeds us the greatest meal, His own Body and Blood.

Love is the Mark of a Christian
Luke 6:27-38

Mother Theresa once said, "I am a pencil in the hand of God that He uses to write love letters to the world." She was saying, "Love is the mark of a Christian."

Luke's gospel gives us an overall picture of Jesus' teachings: love and compassion, forgiveness and reconciliation. Verses like "*Love your enemies*;" and "*Bless those who curse you*" seem to be the opposite of what our culture teaches us: "Don't be a sucker"; "It's a dog-eat-dog world out there"; "Don't let anyone push you around"; "Take them to court."

Christianity is a "love" religion, but is it possible to live this way today? You might say, "Show me someone in this day and age that does it." These verses contain some of the toughest teachings of Christianity, but we do have modern role models, some famous and some not so famous; perhaps some right in our own families. For example, Pope John Paul II visiting his assailant in prison, offering him forgiveness and reconciliation. Perhaps you know of less famous examples.

Loving people live by different standards. What about us? It's not so impossible. We can begin by taking small steps to melt the hardness in our hearts, maybe toward someone who has offended us; we can say a prayer for that someone, asking God to forgive him, asking God to help us forgive; we can be the one to reach out with a call, a note, a little gesture of kindness, an offer to reconcile, even if it was their fault. Martin Luther King said, "…the forgiving act must always be initiated by the person who has been wronged."

The heart of Jesus' teachings is love, and authentic Christian love has its own rules. They may not be logical; they may not make "common sense." It may not be easy. But love, unconditional love, is the mark of a Christian.

We could pray: "Heavenly Father, open our hearts to all humanity. Let us be slow to judgment and quick to forgiveness. Give us patience, empathy, and love. Amen."

May you make your mark as a Christian!

By Our Fruits They Will Know Us

Luke 6: 39-45

In 2001, on a mission trip to build a children's hospice in Hondurans, I worked with two natives who appeared rather rough, and who spoke only Spanish.

My 1st impression was, "Oh, brother, what are we in for? Who's going to show us what to do?" How quick I was to misjudge! These men were artisans at mixing mortar and building concrete block walls. They patiently taught us, and soon, we were kidding around. We could see the sincerity in their eyes and in their smiles we could see the love of Christ.

In the gospel of Luke, we read, "By their fruits you shall know them." Do you suppose that means, "By our fruits they will know *us*?"

Jesus uses the image of a tree and its fruit. He says, "*...every tree is known by its own fruit...*" Who are the "trees?" We are! What is the "fruit?" It's the quality of our speech and the quality of our actions.

It seems so easy to solve everyone else's problems. When we point a finger at another person, at least three fingers are pointing back at us. Psychologists tell us that the faults of other people that bother us the most are the faults we see in ourselves. "By our fruits they will know us."

Our speech can reveal our faults or our virtues. What's in our hearts comes out in our speech. Others can easily see what's happening inside us. Maybe it's money and material things; maybe its off-color stories or bad language or gossip. Or maybe it's the goodness in others. "By our fruits they will know us."

Psychologists also tell us that what we think determines how we act. We choose our behavior. Our choices of friends and our choices of mentors have a lot to do with how we act. We can choose that special teacher, or someone at school or at work - someone we really admire, someone we want to imitate. Over time we can get closer to them, and then we can

Deacon Anthony C. Bonacci   125

learn from them. Jesus says, *"No disciple is superior to the teacher; but when fully trained, every disciple will be like his teacher."* "By our fruits they will know us."

Our Bishop Emeritus, James A. Griffin, is a great homilist, and a great writer. During Lent, he uses the term, "metanoia," which means a change of heart. That's what Jesus is concerned with in this gospel: metanoia, within you and within me. Jesus is saying, "Look within your own hearts, look at your own behavior, not the other person's ...fill your hearts with goodness; nourish it with the Word; nourish it with the Eucharist; nourish it with quality speech, and with quality actions."

Jesus asks us to refrain from judging others; to choose good mentors; to change our hearts and improve the quality of our speech and our actions.

Jesus speaks to us. We are His disciples, and He is counting on us.

May you bear good fruit!

Jesus - Gentle But Demanding
Luke 9:51-62

"God has more for you to do." This is the comment I received on a "get well" card from my graduate school advisor after my heart attack at the age of 44. He said that I needed to take better care of myself, and that family and friends who loved me were counting on me.

If you're alive, God has more for you to do.

In the gospel of Luke, Jesus had a lot to do. Notice His call; His call to *follow* Him: It's a gentle call, but a demanding call.

Notice the people's responses to His call: first, the Samaritans who won't even listen to Him; they're prejudiced against Him. Jesus understands, forgives, and moves on. He shows us a gentle, non-violent response.

Then, we have three people who wish to follow Jesus: sincere people, busy people, like us. Maybe we're like the first man, who says enthusiastically, "I will follow You wherever, Lord!" And Jesus gently says, "Great, but do you realize what a difficult life this is? Being my disciple is no life of leisure. It's tough, it's sacrificial..." Maybe we're like the second man. Jesus gently says, "*Follow Me.*" And we say, "Great, Lord. But you know, I've got to hang around here for about twenty years, until I'm financially secure. Then I'll be ready to follow You. Don't call me, I'll call You...." And Jesus gently says, "Being my disciple means being unselfish, non-materialistic, actively ministering to others."

Or maybe we're like the third man: "I'll follow you, Lord. But I've got plans, you know? I've got places to go, people to see, and then maybe..." And Jesus gently says, "Nothing is more important than following Me."

It's tough to be His disciple. A Franciscan priest at the University of Steubenville once said, "Christianity is highly inconvenient!" It's true. We have cares and concerns (jobs, children, aging parents, house, car, etc.). It's difficult to put God first in our lives. But we are called to follow Him and to serve Him above any self-interest or worldly interest. Jesus is gentle, but Jesus is demanding.

So how do we do it? How do we handle the everyday stuff, and yet keep God first in our life? How do we form an unselfish attitude when all around us our society says, "Get what you want!; Do what feels good!; Let the other guy earn his own slice of the pie! The person with the most toys, wins!" (Did you ever see a hearse pulling a U-haul trailer?)

There once was a frail but wise old man in Rome with some suggestions; in one of his last encyclicals, St. Pope John Paul II said:

"Be docile to the movement of the Holy Spirit." He's saying, listen for God's prompts in everyday situations. Sometimes they come through a friend or spouse, sometimes they come through a little child, or an older person's needs; sometimes they come through trials that force us to change our ways;

"Learn the art of prayer." He's saying, have a constant conversation with God. When we awaken each morning, we can say, "Thank you, God for another day." When we have to make a tough decision during the day, we can say, "Help me out here, Lord." When we lie on the pillow at night, we can say, "Watch over my loved ones, Lord, those here on this earth, and those there with You..."

"Make the Eucharist the center of your parish life." He's saying, "Value the Eucharist." What a privilege we have as Catholic Christians to hold the body of Christ in our hands; what a privilege to receive Him, absorb Him, into our body and into our hearts.

Jesus is gentle, but Jesus is demanding. He wants to be the center of our life, not just a slot on Sunday mornings. Don't be a punch in, punch out, "Give me my wafer and let me go home" Catholic. Jesus challenges us to follow Him - NOW, not later. Sometimes, there is no later. He challenges us to give of ourselves, to commit fully to Him.

Real Hospitality

Luke 10:38-42

The Martha and Mary story is a story about hospitality. It's a story that sounds familiar; not just the bible story, but the real life story that goes along with it. Some of us would probably admit to being a "Martha:" anxious when having guests, consumed by the preparations, more concerned with the serving than the one being served.

Maybe some of us would admit to being a Mary: "Let's sit on the floor and talk, we can worry about dinner later; maybe we'll make sandwiches." Some of us are born "Marthas;" some of us are born "Marys."

What is real "hospitality?" It means being present to people, giving them our time and attention, and meeting their inter-personal and spiritual needs. It's a form of service; it's a form of ministry. That's why we have usher/greeters; we want everyone to feel welcome.

Right now, think of someone you know, who when you talk with them, gives you all their attention, and you always get the feeling that they really care about you. They see the goodness and wonder of God in you. They look at your goodness and they always accept you, warts and all. What a treasure to know someone like this.

Jesus neither praises nor condemns Martha for her busyness. He doesn't patronize her, either. He gently cautions her about her anxiety. He gently reminds her of the primary importance of hearing what He has to say. He teaches Martha *and us* that our actions must have a deeper meaning.

Mary simply enjoys Jesus' presence. She wanted to hear the Word of God. She wants to meditate on His message. All her interest and attention is directed to Him.

Jesus loved both Martha and Mary. But He didn't care about the details of the meal. He didn't care if the meal was late. His priority is the people He is with.

Deacon Anthony C. Bonacci

Martha was a good woman, trying to be a good hostess. She simply forgot why hospitality is important. Mary was a good hostess, too. But her response to Christ was Faith, Faith as St. John Paul II defined it: "Giving oneself totally to God, and striving always to do God's will." Relaxed and sitting at Jesus' feet, Mary's first priority is listening to His words.

Some years ago, there was a young man who loved to host parties. He liked to impress his friends and co-workers with home-made foods. But he was so concerned to have everything perfect, that he spent most of his time in the kitchen. He came out only a few seconds at a time, smiling at his guests as he served trays of food. At the end of the party, he realized he hadn't even spoken with most of his guests, and he still had the clean-up to do. He had missed the enjoyment of the people, the conversation, the laughing, and the whole purpose of the gathering.

Eventually, the young man came to realize that real "hospitality" meant being present to his guests, listening and sharing life stories with them, and seeing the goodness and wonder of God in them.

Real hospitality helps us live the two great commandments: love of God and love of neighbor. Love of God motivates us to *love* others. Jesus' Word and Jesus' teachings motivate us to *serve* others, to minister to others, and most of all, to be present to others. The challenge for us is to focus on the "why" of hospitality, to focus on the one being served. Hospitality, like everything we do, must have a deeper meaning, a meaning that reaches beyond this life, to the kingdom of heaven.

May we show real hospitality to others.

Prayer Changes Things

Luke 11:1-13

In the gospel of Luke, we find Jesus at prayer. Jesus prayed before all the important events of His life, and before He made big decisions, like choosing His apostles. He prayed before He set out on His last journey to Jerusalem, and He prayed in the Garden of Gethsemane before His passion and death. Jesus knew that prayer changes things.

In this gospel, Jesus teaches us how to pray - not so much what to pray for, but HOW to pray. He tells us to ask and keep asking, to be *persistent*, like the man knocking on his neighbor's door. Then Jesus tells us that God the Father gives His children only good things, like any loving father.

When we talk to God, like a child talking to his father with trust and openness, we get an honest picture of our real motives in life. What do I want out of life? Why do I choose and act as I do? What's really important to me?

Through prayer, we see our obligations to others - family, friends, coworkers, other students. We come to understand our personal role in life. What is God asking of me?

Jesus knew that prayer changes things. As Christians, we know that prayer changes things. It's true. Sometimes, a prayer seems to bring an answer that we don't expect or don't like, because God is asking for a change in our lives, a response that is good for us.

As parents, we should teach our children how to pray, and let them talk to Jesus in their own words, like a brother, for that's who He is. We can remind them that God the Father only gives us good things, that He is not a harsh and cruel God. We can teach them that suffering is not a punishment; that prayer helps us understand why bad things can happen to good people, and that the Eucharist gives us the strength to deal with the trials, sufferings, and disappointments that are part of life. Above all, we can teach them that prayer changes things!

Note Jesus' quote: *"Ask and you shall receive..."* Jesus does not say that we will receive *exactly* what we seek. But God surely answers prayer - in His own time and in His own way. Sometimes the answer is "Yes," sometimes it's "No," and sometimes it's "Later." The challenge for us is to persevere in prayer. God always responds to our prayer in ways that are best for us. God wants the best for us, which ultimately is the gift of the Holy Spirit, the gift of His Divine Presence among us and within us.

Rich in What Matters to God

On a certain PBS program, they told of a new disease, a disease that seems to be hitting everyone - adults, children, and teenagers. They called it "Affluenza." The symptoms are feelings of overload, debt, anxiety, and stress. It's caused, they said, by our constant pursuit of "MORE!" It's the disease of *Materialism*.

We Americans seem to be totally absorbed with material things; we're always trying to get more "stuff," accumulate more earthly things. It's not the ownership of "things" that's the problem. The real problem is that we tend to identify with our stuff. For many, our self-esteem is associated with what we own. We buy more and more "stuff" to elevate our status in our own eyes or in the eyes of others. We compare what we have with what "they" have. Jesus says, *"Take care to guard against all greed, for though one may be rich, one's life does not consist of possessions."* He's saying, "avoid identifying yourselves with what you have."

Materialism offers false promises: consider how many choices we have in our stores.

Materialism offers a false sense of security: things will eventually rust or wear out.

Materialism can break up families. In almost every family, there's an estrangement of a family member because of an inheritance – money or things.

Materialism adds to our stress level, because we have to store things, maintain them, secure them, and insure them. Sometimes the things we think we own, own us.

Jesus quotes God the Father saying, *"You fool, this night your life will be demanded of you, and the things you have accumulated, to whom will they*

Deacon Anthony C. Bonacci   133

belong?" He adds, *"Thus will it be for all who store up treasure for themselves but are not rich in what matters to God."*

Materialism can distract us from knowing and trusting in God, from trying to get rich in what matters to God. That's where real wealth is; that's where true wealth is.

To get rich in what matters to God:

First, put God first: reflect on the many blessings we already have, and recognize that our material things are a blessing and a gift from God.

Second, set our minds on things above, not on the things of earth. We are more than what we have. We need to free ourselves from identifying with our stuff.

Then we can put more emphasis on our spiritual life: on getting our priorities straight, devoting ourselves to things that will last, seeking God's will, and using our earthly possessions to do God's work. That's how we get rich in what matters to God.

Many years ago, I was executor of a dear relative's estate, and as I walked though her house after her funeral, I thought, "What good is all this stuff when God calls you?" Someday, every one of us will be called by God. We'll have to give up every THING we have. You and I will be judged on how "rich" we are - how rich in what matters to God.

A Casual Acquaintance Is Not Good Enough

Luke 13:22-30

Teaching is a tough job. In Luke's gospel, we see Jesus as teacher. And He has a tough lesson. Jesus is teaching us about heaven. He sounds harsh; He says there's a "narrow gate," and it takes great effort to get through the "narrow gate." Jesus says, *"Strive to enter..."* He describes the "outsiders," trying to convince Him that they were His friends here on earth. But He tells them He doesn't know them, He tells them to *"Depart..."*

Jesus is telling us that a casual acquaintance with Him is not good enough. He says the "outsiders" will anguish when they see who's inside. As Mother Angelica once said, "There's going to be some surprises in heaven. Some people we don't expect to find in the kingdom will be there, and some who think they're going to be there, won't be."

A lady once told me how she thinks about heaven. She said "We work so hard in high school and college, striving to get that diploma, that degree; we work hard at our marriage and our friendships, striving to develop good relationships; we strive at sports, doing our best to win. If we're building a deck, we have an exact plan; we strive to cut each piece perfectly. How we strive for these things - what effort we expend! Maybe we should strive harder to get to heaven!?" This woman realized that a casual acquaintance with Jesus isn't good enough.

Maybe we should ask ourselves, "Am I getting a little casual in my faith, in my worshipping, in how I receive the Eucharist? Am I taking Jesus for granted?"

If Jesus was standing before us, He would likely say,

"My dear brothers and sisters: Salvation is open to all; heaven is attainable - but guard against a passive or casual faith; Your journey is under way - there will be trials in this life (I told you there would be), but grace comes with

tribulation; it brings you closer to Me. Focus on what lies ahead - this life isn't all there is. Take to heart the lessons of the Scriptures - accept my teachings as the Word of God, and put them into practice. When you receive Me in the Eucharist, allow Me to transform your life - It's not just a wafer! It's my body and blood!"

"Most of all, dearest ones, I want a personal, intimate relationship with you. A casual acquaintance is not good enough. The 'narrow gate' I speak of, is ME! I AM the gate!"

Jesus challenges us to commit totally to the goal; the goal of everlasting life. It takes a effort; it takes discipline. And here's a little secret: the effort can be just as enjoyable as the goal. Get into the life of the Church: serve as an usher/greeter, lector, server, Extraordinary Minister of the Eucharist, or religion teacher.

Jesus invites us to the banquet: the Eucharist we receive today, and the heavenly banquet yet to come. The invitation is open, but only those who totally respond, will be admitted.

Believe it. A casual acquaintance is not good enough.

"The Cost of Discipleship"

Luke 14:25-33

Our religion teachers strive to teach the faith and hand on the faith to our young people. They teach the children the meaning of "disciple" - one who follows another. In the gospel of Luke, Jesus asks *us* to be His disciples, to follow Him.

They teach the children what "commitment" means - an agreement or promise. Jesus asks *us* for a commitment to Him, and only Him. He tells two parables about "counting the cost," He's really asking us, "Do you know what you're getting yourself into?"

Our religion teachers explain the word "detachment" - a separation or withdrawal. Jesus tells us that if we want to be His disciples, we must detach ourselves from worldly possessions.

Another word the children learn is "priority" - a precedence or superiority. Jesus makes it clear that He demands priority in our lives, even above our loved ones.

Luke's gospel is about the meaning of discipleship, and the cost of discipleship. Jesus says, *"Whoever does not carry his own cross and come after me cannot be my disciple."* The Lord is asking us to follow Him as a disciple, to commit totally to Him, to detach ourselves from worldly possessions, and even ourselves; to give Him priority above even those closest to us; and then says there are crosses, too?

And our Lord says, *"Yes; I know what it's like; I was a human once, remember? Look what they did to me!"*

The most difficult part of being a disciple is accepting the crosses and bearing the sufferings and setbacks that happen: the unfortunate accident, the unexplainable loss of a healthy child, the unfair loss of a job, the undeserved diagnosis of a life-threatening illness, or the loneliness of becoming a widow or widower. These are things that have happened to the

Deacon Anthony C. Bonacci 137

people around us. And these crosses are often a mystery: unexplainable, unfair, and undeserved. The truth is, we won't understand their meaning until we reach the other side. One thing is for sure: these crosses have to do with detachment from self. As one famous preacher said, "Don't run from the Cross…embrace it!" The cross identifies us as disciples.

Discipleship is not easy. Discipleship is not cheap. It's costly. Being a Christian is a combination of blessings and sufferings; a combination of promise (eternal life) - and crosses in this life (guaranteed). Always remember (and this is the good news), our fellowship with God and others grows in the process.

Every day, Jesus invites us to follow Him, to be His disciple.

Sharing Worldly Wealth

Luke 16: 1-13

I once knew of a family who bought a new house. They were very proud of their new house. It had new furniture and new carpet; the children had their own bedrooms; there were several bathrooms, a two-car garage, and a nice yard.

Not long after they moved in, they heard about another family with serious trouble at home. The problems were so serious that the mother and children of the other family needed a safe place to stay. The family with the new house took in this mother and children, shared their new house, their food, and whatever they had with the broken family. They took care of them until other arrangements could be made.

I still admire this generous family. I remember asking myself, "Could I do that? Would I do that?" Would I share my new home, all my worldly wealth, with "strangers?" Or would I say, "Well, they should call the Welfare Department, or somebody!"

In the gospel of Luke, we read the parable of the "unjust steward." Some call him the "shrewd manager." This man had been playing fast and loose with his boss' property, and was about to be fired. So he uses shrewdness to protect his future. Jesus says that even the man's boss admired his ingenuity.

Jesus is suggesting that we use our imagination to further God's kingdom, not in a dishonest way, but by being resourceful in the way we use material things. God has given us so much! Most of us have a higher standard of living than our parents; more food, clothing, and living space than we need. Each of us has unique ways to share what we have.

Sometimes, we *want* to share our worldly wealth, but we hesitate, because we want to feel "in control." Our possessions create the illusion of control. And isn't it true, the more we have, the more we want?

Sometimes, we may think, "The needy don't appreciate what we do for them...they're just lazy, shiftless people...let them to go out and get a job!"

I once volunteered with a lady at a soup kitchen. When this lady saw the faces of discouraged, sick, or addicted clients saying, "Look at me, I'm a mess; how can anyone love me? How can God ever love me," she looked at the rest of the servers and said, "Who am I? – that I'm on this side of the counter?"

In this gospel, Jesus is telling us to use our worldly wealth for eternal benefit; that this world's goods will fail us; that we should use our worldly wealth to benefit others. Jesus is telling us that using our worldly wealth wisely advances us spiritually.

In this difficult time for our country and its leaders, God's Word is telling us to re-evaluate our use of wealth and power. God's Word is telling us it's time for moral renewal, individually, and as a country.

The challenge for us is to be alert in using what God has given us; the opportunities pass so quickly!

The challenge for us is to be generous; to follow our hearts, like the family with the new house.

When we approach the Eucharist, let us thank God for what we have, and ask ourselves, "Does this next *thing* that I want, does this next *action* I am about to take: does it further the kingdom of God? Does it bring me closer to my neighbor? Does it bring me closer to my God?

Give Him Thanks and Praise

Luke 17: 11-19

A young man was watching his 80-year old neighbor planting a small peach tree. He asked him, "Sir, you surely don't expect to be eating peaches from that tree, do you?" The old man stopped and rested on the shovel. He said, "No, son, at my age I know I won't. But all my life I've enjoyed peaches... never from a tree I planted myself... I'm just trying to say 'thanks' to the people who planted the trees for me." The old man is expressing *gratitude*.

Luke's gospel story is about gratitude. It's the story about ten lepers who were cured by Jesus. Nine of them continued on their journey, and only one returned to thank Him.

Can you imagine the disappointment and sadness in Jesus' voice: *"Where are the other nine?"* Jesus' heart had gone out to them, yet only one came back, praising God, and thanking Jesus for the cure.

Maybe the nine had reasons for not saying "thanks." Maybe they got so excited about being cured that they forgot.

Maybe they thought that Jesus was just "doing His job" as "that miracle worker from Nazareth."

Maybe they were just out to exploit Jesus, to get what they could from Him ?

This gospel stirs us to ask, "Am I ungrateful?" We don't want to be. We're so busy, maybe we just forget?

Maybe we think God's just doing His job?

Maybe sometimes we "exploit" God; we only go to Him, we only need Him when we're in trouble!

On the other hand, there are many ways we can and do show gratitude. For example, when we return a favor; when we send a "thank you" note for a gift or a kind gesture; when we say grace before meals; or when we respond to the needs of others, out of gratitude to God for what He's given us!

We show gratitude when we worship with others. The Mass is our Eucharist! "Eucharist" means "thanksgiving." Like the leper who came back, we come to a sacred place to "praise God in a loud voice;" like the leper who came back, we "kneel at the feet of Jesus, giving Him thanks."

At every Mass, we hear the priest say, "It is right always and everywhere to give You thanks!" There's the challenge! Real gratitude doesn't depend on the circumstances. Real thankfulness is an attitude of soul, a readiness always to give thanks. It's an attitude of heart that senses everything in life as a gift.

Gratitude may be expressed for a new baby, or good health, or a decent job; or the love of a good friend, a good marriage, and a supportive family. Sometimes, it's giving thanks for the life of a loved one who's passed on, and how their life enriched our life. Sometimes, it's saying, "Thank you God, for that difficulty, for that set-back that I took so hard. But with your help, I got through it, and now I see how it made me stronger, now I see why you brought that special person into my life; now I see how that difficulty brought me closer to You."

We are never alone in our journey toward God: sometimes He's ahead, leading; sometimes, He's behind, pushing; sometimes, He's alongside, accompanying; and sometimes, as many of us have experienced, He carries us. God is always on the road to meet us, and a proper relationship with God includes *gratitude*. We need to say thanks.

May we be like the grateful leper, who couldn't think of his blessings without thinking of God, and who couldn't think of God without offering Him thanks.

Recognizing the King

Luke 23: 35-43

At the end of the church year, in thousands of churches around the world, Christians celebrate a very special day we call "Christ the King" Sunday.

"Christ the King:" What image does that bring to your mind?

Maybe it's the image from Christian art, the majestic Jesus sitting on a throne, wearing purple robes and a gold crown, surrounded by the angels and saints.

But that's not the image of Jesus in the gospels: the humble Nazorean who sat and ate with sinners, the sick, the poor, and the outcasts. It's not the Jesus in this gospel from Luke: Jesus on the cross, being mocked by the Jewish leaders, the soldiers, and even one of the criminals crucified beside Him. How is this "Christ the King?"

Jesus had told Pilate, *"My kingdom is not of this world."* But Pilate and the others didn't get it! Jesus' *throne* was the cross; His *crown* was a ring of thorny branches. The *robe* thrown over His shoulders was to mock Him. His "army" was twelve ordinary men. Instead of *dominating* others, He *served* others.

Christ is our King, today; He leads us, He protects us, He guides us through the problems, worries, and anxieties of everyday life.

We could offer prayers of thanksgiving every day as our King helps us and guides us on our journey: "Thank you, Lord, for my troubles and trials; they bring me closer to You."

Our Holy Father Francis says, "Let Jesus enter your life, welcome Him as a friend, with TRUST."

If He's our King, we trust Him to help us, to guide us, and to protect us. If He's our King, we obey His rules; we strive to know His will and do His will. If He's our King, we follow His teachings.

If He's our King, we repent. We tell Him we're truly sorry for our sins, and we resolve to do better. We reconcile with God and with the people we've hurt, perhaps an estranged son or daughter or sibling or in-law we haven't spoken to in months, or even years.

If He's our King, we swallow our pride and ask forgiveness. If He's our King, we "let by-gones be by-gones" and forgive him or her for what they did or said. If He's our King, we try to see the pressure the other person is under, and the baggage they might be carrying; we try harder to understand each other; we try to communicate better, and we try to be kinder to each other.

We should ask ourselves: "Is Jesus my king? Is He ruler of my heart?" When we receive Him in the Eucharist, we should   let's pray like the good thief: "Jesus, remember me when you enter upon your reign." And when our time comes, may Christ the King respond to us as He did to the good thief: *"I assure you, this day you will be with me in Paradise."*

May God bless you and those you love; may you have love and peace in Christ the King!

ABOUT THE AUTHOR

Deacon Anthony C. Bonacci is Assistant Dean Emeritus, College of Pharmacy, The Ohio State University. He is the father of four adult children, Lynn Marie (Chapman), Tina Marie (Hardin), Maria Margaret (Lentz), and Anthony G. Bonacci. Deacon Bonacci has been a member of Saint Joseph the Worker parish, Plain City, Ohio, for 49 years, and an ordained deacon for the Diocese of Columbus, Ohio, for 23 years.

He was married to his wife Elaine for 53 years until her untimely passing in 2019. Deacon Bonacci has eight grandchildren ranging in age from 29 years of age to five years of age. He has published articles in *Marriage Encounter* magazine, *Deacon Digest* magazine, *The Catholic Times* of Columbus, *The American Journal of Hospital Pharmacy*, *Tetrahedron Letters*, and local newsletters of the *Marriage Encounter* and *Cursillo* movements.

Reflections for Everyday Life